Guardians of the Eighth Sea

A

History

of the

U. S. Coast Guard
on the

Great Lakes

by

T. Michael O'Brien
Photojournalist First Class
United States Coast Guard

University Press of the Pacific
Honolulu, Hawaii

Guardians of the Eighth Sea: A History of the U. S.
Coast Guard on the Great Lakes

by
T. Michael O'Brien

ISBN: 0-89875-649-9

Reprinted from the 1976 edition

University Press of the Pacific
Honolulu, Hawaii
http://www.universitypressofthepacific.com

TO THOSE WHO SERVED

FOREWORD

Throughout the United States, local residents customarily view their hometown U. S. Coast Guard units as intimate parts of the civilian community. Nowhere is this truer than in the Great Lakes region. Here, for almost 200 years, the lives of the people and Coast Guardsmen have been intermingled in a most special bond.

As enterprising Americans pressed westward along the southern shores of these primeval lakes and upon them, aids to navigation in the form of lighthouses and buoys, and armed revenue cutters were promptly provided by the Federal Government to facilitate their progress. Other varied services of the entity destined to become known as the U. S. Coast Guard, whether lifesaving stations, inspections of steam vessels or regulation of navigational waterways, were provided as needs arose, until today, the Service is ubiquitous on the Inland Seas. Certainly, here, the U. S. Coast Guard has no problem with public awareness about its multifaceted missions in the service of humanity.

The following historical narrative will serve not only to enlighten present-day Americans to the vital services performed by the U. S. Coast Guard, but also, as a permanent record, will benefit generations to follow. By researching and publishing this history, the Ninth Coast Guard District could have performed no more appropriate service in commemoration of our Nation's Bicentennial Year. This work reflects the essence of the Coast Guard today, as well as its distinguished and heroic past. No doubt Coast Guardsmen in the national celebrations to come, in 50 or 100 years, will look back at this permanent record as one to emulate.

As one who was born and reared within the range of the piercing "steamboat whistles" on the Inland Seas, I can, personally, state that a reading of this history brought back many nostalgic memories and provided a new awareness of the intertwining of the history of the Great Lakes Region and that of the uniquely humanitarian-oriented military service, the Coast Guard.

In my opinion, this highly worthy project reflects the deep emotion that all Americans feel in this Bicentennial Year.

Truman R. Strobridge
U. S. Coast Guard Historian
U. S. Coast Guard Headquarters

PREFACE

Conceived as a maritime customs enforcement unit in the fledgling days of our nation, the United States Coast Guard has grown and developed in its one hundred and eighty-six years of existence into a uniquely humanitarian military institution. An amalgamation of several federal agencies, today's Coast Guard continues to develop and expand in many areas, earning an enviable reputation as the forerunner in such fields as Search and Rescue, Boating Safety, and Marine Environmental Protection.

In the Great Lakes Region, the Coast Guard's predecessors expanded and developed with the area itself, becoming an integral part of the history and the greatness of the region. Our existence today is the result of the accomplishments of generations of men and women who served. It is their story which we present here.

James S. Gracey
Rear Admiral, United States Coast Guard
Commander,
Ninth Coast Guard District

CONTENTS

ACKNOWLEDGEMENTS

This publication was the product of a team effort, with the author as the central figure. He was responsible for the actual research and writing of the manuscript, selecting the illustrations and compiling the appendices and bibliography. In addition to his on duty time, he spent many hours of his own time on the production of this book.

A considerable amount of effort was provided by PA2 Kenneth L. Randall, Jr., PA3 James E. Vickerman and SN David Laird, who spent innumerable hours copying and printing photographs for the book, and Mrs. Carolyn S. Linville who patiently typed and retyped the manuscript.

The Public Affairs Office acknowledges with pleasure the invaluable assistance of Truman R. Strobridge, without whose encouragement and knowledge this work could not have been completed; Dr. Julius F. Wolff, Jr., Professor of Political Science, University of Minnesota; Dennis L. Noble, author of many articles on the Great Lakes; Mr. Allan Quinn of the Cleveland Public Library; Mrs. Hope Holdcamper and Mr. William Sherman of the National Archives; Mr. James Woodward of the Great Lakes Historical Society; Mrs. William Harris of the Michigan City, Indiana Historical Society; Mr. William Lee of the Dossin Great Lakes Museum; The Evanston Historical Society; Mr. John Packard of the Lake Carriers Association and Mrs. Betty Segedi of the Still Picture Branch at Coast Guard Headquarters.

A final note of thanks goes to Rear Admiral James S. Gracey and Captain Herbert E. Lindemann for their trust and support. Without their support, this work would not have been possible.

Daniel F. Shotwell
Lieutenant,
United States Coast Guard
Public Affairs Officer,
Ninth Coast Guard District

CHAPTER I

THE REVENUE CUTTER SERVICE

The precursor of today's Coast Guard was known by several titles during the period 1790-1915. It never had a statutory designation although as early as 1832 the Secretary of the Treasury referred to it as the "Revenue-Cutter Service". Official documents of this early period also made reference to it as the "Revenue

Alexander Hamilton, first Secretary of the Treasury and considered by some to be the father of the U. S. Coast Guard.

Service", "Revenue Marine", "Revenue-Marine Service", and "the system of cutters". Until 1863 no specific references were made to the Service in any statutes. In that year, an act (12 Stat. L., 639) called it the "United States Revenue-Cutter Service." This term was later adopted in the Revised Statutes but did not become the universally accepted designation until 1894. To avoid confusion we will utilize the term "Revenue Cutter Service" in this work.

Congress recognizing the need for a floating police force approved July 31, 1789 "An act to regulate the collection of duties imposed by law on the tonnage of ships or vessels, and on goods, wares, and merchandises imported into

the United States." The act provided for each port to have a surveyor whose duties would include "the employment of the boats which may be provided for securing the collection of the revenue" (I Stat. L., 29, 37). No provision, however, was made for the boats themselves. In fact, it was not until August 4, 1790 that construction and equipment of the cutters were authorized. Since, at this time, the new nation had no navy, the Service was placed under the control of the Treasury Department where it re-

Gilbert Knapp

mained until 1967 when it was reorganized into the Department of Transportation.

We do not know certainly when the predecessors of the Coast Guard came to the Great Lakes. Scholars and historians have made many guesses and there seems to be a general agreement that somewhere between 1809 and 1820 both the Lighthouse Service and the Revenue Cutter Service extended their activities to the area. This relative inaccessibility of the necessary information—even though compensated

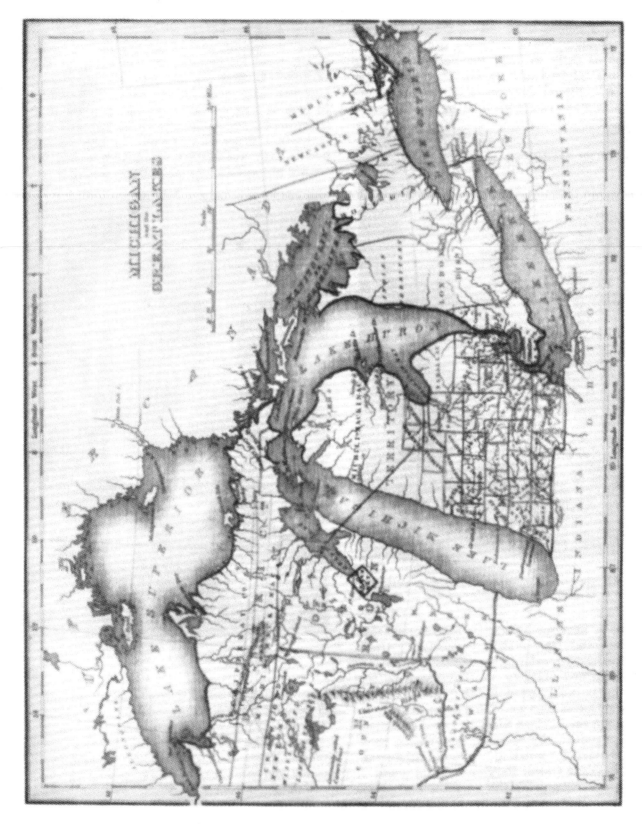

U. S. Great Lakes Region, 1835.

4

for to some extent, by non-official investigations—may help to explain why certain segments of this work seem vague and incomplete.

There is no really convincing evidence of a Coast Guard presence on the Great Lakes until 1818. It was in this year, that the first lighthouses were established. This same year, the Rush-Bagot Agreement was approved. A direct result of the War of 1812, the agreement provided that the United States and Canada would limit their vessels of war on the Great Lakes to four each, none exceeding 100 tons and armed only with one eighteen-pounder while all other armed vessels on the Lakes were to be dismantled and no others were to be built or armed except those needed for revenue control. The wording of this agreement lends credence to the theory that revenue cutters were operating on the Great Lakes prior to the War of 1812. Indeed, biographical data concerning Captain Gilbert Knapp compiled in the two WPA biographical sketches of Gilbert Knapp written circa 1940 make reference to him as Captain of the Revenue Cutter ALEXANDER J. DALLAS, homeported in Detroit, Michigan as early as May 1819. Further mention of Knapp and his cutter is made by Henry R. Schoolcraft in his *Narrative Journal of Travels Through the Northwestern Regions of the United States Extending from Detroit through the Great Chain of American Lakes to the Sources of the Mississippi River in the Year 1820*. Mansfield's *History of the Great Lakes* also alludes to a Revenue Cutter FAIRPLAY sailing into Chicago Harbor prior to 1819. There are no official documents to corroborate these testimonies, a fact we consider of relative unimportance due to the almost total absence of official documents prior to 1833. What we do feel is significant, however, is that a representative presence of the Revenue Cutter Service had been established on the Lakes and at least unofficially documented prior to 1820.

The first official document we could locate which acknowledged the existence of a Revenue Cutter being assigned to the Great Lakes was the assignment in 1829 of Captain Daniel Dobbins to the Revenue Cutter stationed at Presque Isle on the Pennsylvania shore of Lake Erie. Dobbins, one of the Lakes most illustrious folk heroes became Captain of the Revenue Cutter ERIE in 1832 when she was completed. ERIE made her first voyage April 29th 1833 when she proceeded to the port of Cleveland, Ohio.

Four years earlier, in 1829, Andrew Jackson had begun his tenure as President of the United States and one of his first steps had been to remove any political opponents from public office, replacing them with his supporters. Jackson's extension of the so-called "spoils system" had brought politics into the range of the average man and encouraged many individuals to look upon the public payroll as a trough where they could gorge themselves at taxpayers' expense. This policy coupled with rising federal tariff laws and South Carolina's threatened secession left all government agencies open prey for the administration's enemies. That the Revenue Cutter Service was no exception is well illustrated by Thomas Forster's letter to Secretary of the Treasury William Duane dated September 7th 1833. In his letter, Forster, who was Collector of Customs for the Presque Isle District, staunchly defends the crew of ERIE against charges of intemperance by unknown character assassins who, according to Forster ". . .would not wince at traducing the character and standing of any person favourable to the present administration. . ." Sometime later, Forster's own son, a lighthouse keeper, was charged with intemperance and dereliction of duty as a result of intoxication. Throughout the Jacksonian Era, anti-administrationists constantly sought the removal of all pro-Jackson officials.

Between May 1837 and November 1838 two insurrections broke out in Canada. Known as the Papineau-Mackenzie Rebellion, after the principle antagonists, the insurgents found much sympathy and encouragement in the United States, especially in the state of New York. At one point, 700 armed men crossed over to Navy Island on the Canadian side of the Niagara River, seizing it and establishing a base to be used for launching an invasion of the Canadian mainland. United States-Great Britain relations were seriously threatened and the President issued a Proclamation of Neutrality prohibiting American citizens from interfering with the internal affairs of Canada. To enforce this policy the U. S. Army under General Wool was sent to the Niagara Frontier assisted by the Revenue Cutter ERIE. The revolution failed and order was restored, thus freeing ERIE for resumption of her revenue collecting duties. On June 12, 1849 ERIE was put up for sale and on July 13 was bought for $700.00.

It will be of interest here to give a brief account of the life of Daniel Dobbins, Captain of the ERIE. Born, one day after the new nation, on July 5, 1776 at Lewistown, Pennsylvania, he was among the party of surveyors who laid out the town of Erie in 1796. After marrying Mary

Daniel Dobbins

West of Carlisle, Pennsylvania in 1800, he returned to Erie where he accepted his first command on the Lakes as part-owner and master of the schooner *Harlequin*. Between 1803 and 1809 he sailed the schooners *Good Intent*, *Wilkinson*, and *Ranger*. In 1809 he, and Rufus S. Reed purchased the schooner *Charlotte*, refitted her into a two topsail schooner and changed her name to *Salina*. It was aboard the *Salina* that Captain Dobbins first become involved in the War of 1812. While lying at anchor off Mackinaw with over $200,000 worth of furs aboard, the *Salina* was surprised and captured by a fleet of British gunboats. That vessel and a second schooner, *Mary*, were dis-

patched as cartels and upon arrival at Detroit were seized by General Hull, commander of the American forces. Detroit, however, also fell and the *Salina* again became a British prize. This time Dobbins escaped and worked his way back to Erie where he reported the news of Detroit's capture to General Mead who sent him on to President Madison. As a result of this trip to Washington, Madison commissioned him a Sailing Master in the United States Navy and returned him to Erie. Dobbins' accomplishments in providing Commodore Perry with a fleet are quite well documented in numerous sources so we will not dwell on them. After the war, Dobbins served in many capacities until 1829 when President Jackson appointed him a Captain in the Revenue Cutter Service and placed him in command of the Revenue Cutter RICHARD RUSH in New York. As mentioned earlier, when Jackson became President, he ousted all his known opponents from positions in government. Captain Gilbert Knapp, who, as mentioned earlier, commanded the only revenue cutter on the Lakes at this time, was an outspoken opponent of the "Frontiersman President" and after making some rather derogatory remarks on Election Day in Erie, he was promptly dismissed on April 4, 1829 making room for Dobbins. The two Captains would trade jobs with each succeeding administration's takeover. When Harrison ascended to the Presidency, Knapp replaced Dobbins. Then positions were reversed when Polk came into office. Finally, on May 9, 1849 President Zachary Taylor revoked Dobbins' commission again and he retired. He died at Erie on February 29, 1856 at the age of eighty. Twenty-three years later, his wife Mary died at the age of 100 years. As we will see later, the Dobbins family continued to carry on a tradition of public service, long after the death of Daniel Dobbins.

Despite his apparent rivalry with Dobbins for command of revenue cutters, Gilbert Knapp also made many worthwhile contributions during the early history of the Lakes. Knapp was a native of Cape Cod, Massachusetts. Born in Chatham on December 3, 1790, he first went to sea at age 15. During the War of 1812 he served as Master's Mate on the *Leo*, a privateer chartered by the government to carry dispatches to France. In May of 1819 he received his commission in the Revenue Cutter Service and took command of the cutter serving the

Great Lakes. For ten years he served without incident until his already described politically engendered replacement by Dobbins. During the Jackson administration Knapp decided to take advantage of the rapid expansion westward and in 1833 after a treaty had been reached with the Indians he began his plan for development of a townsite. Although he named the site Port Gilbert, it later was renamed Racine, Wisconsin when a post office was established there. While serving on the Rump Council of the Territory of Wisconsin from 1836-1838, events in Washington were taking place which would return Captain Knapp to the Revenue Cutter Service.

After Zachary Taylor's final revocation of Daniel Dobbins' commission Captain Knapp returned again to the Revenue Cutter Service but in 1853 when the Service reduced its number of officers, his commission was revoked and he returned to Racine. After serving in the Wisconsin legislature he volunteered his services again when the Civil War broke out and was recommissioned May 3, 1861. He served on the cutters DOBBIN, FLOYD and MORRIS before returning to the Great Lakes in March of 1865 when he supervised the construction of two sidewheel steamers, FESSENDEN and SHERMAN. He assumed command of SHERMAN in November 1865. SHERMAN's name was later apparently changed to FESSENDEN. Knapp lost command December 6, 1870 but regained it in May of 1871. His active career ended abruptly in April of 1872 when he was removed from command and placed on "Permanent Waiting Orders" (forerunner of the retired lists which permitted officers to retain a percentage of their pay). He returned to Racine where he died July 31, 1887.

Following the sometimes colorful career of the ERIE came a period when the Revenue Cutter Service faded into efficient obscurity, performing its assigned duties without much notoriety. Even official records contain little if any information on cutters assigned to the Lakes prior to the Civil War. The most notable cause of this decided absence of information probably was the Service's practice of chartering local vessels for use as cutters rather than building or procuring new ones. During this pre-Civil War period, the Revenue Cutter Service apparently maintained a low profile on the Great Lakes. Whether this was intentional or not is uncertain, but if this was their intention, they were most successful. Local newspapers of the day referring to the vessels reinforced their anonymity, identifying them only as "the local revenue cutter". Even the Treasury Department's *Record of Movements, Vessels of the United States Coast Guard, 1790-December 31, 1933* contains only limited information on Great Lakes cutters. For instance, the entry for the HARRISON, a vessel which served for six years, comprises only six lines and gives little insight into her history except that she was built at Erie, Pennsylvania in 1848, entered service August 14, 1849, was damaged in a gale November 12, 1852 and sold in 1856.

Mansfield's *History of the Great Lakes* mentions briefly that in 1861 five revenue cutters: JACOB THOMPSON, A. V. BROWN, ISAAC TONEY, JEREMIAH S. BLACK, and HOWELL COBB, were ordered to New York, leaving only one cutter on the Lakes. Despite a difference in spelling for the ISAAC TONCEY and the destination, the *Record of Movements* would appear to confirm this report in that the entry for the HOWELL COBB on December 18, 1861 states, "Arrived at Boston in company with the BROWN, BLACK, TONCEY, and THOMPSON." Entries for the other vessels are similar. Four of the five were apparently used as replacements for other cutters detailed to blockade and combat duty, for records indicate they spent the entire war in New England waters, the A. V. BROWN rendering important service off the North Carolina coast.

One point of interest is that it was during this pre-war period of the Service's relative obscurity that the first known instance of the use of the term *Coast Guard* was made. Captain Alexander Frazer, the first Commandant, referring to the men and vessels of his service, in his annual report of 1846, described them as "a coast guard in time of war . . ." The term again was used in an editorial published November 26, 1864 in the *Army and Navy Journal* which also contained an early variant of today's Coast Guard's motto: "Keeping always under steam and ever ready, in the event of extraordinary need, to render valuable service, the cutters can be made to form a coast guard whose value it is impossible at the present time to estimate."

The war record of the cutters had brought new acclaim and public recognition for the Revenue Cutter Service. Perhaps the most well-known of the postwar cutters serving on the Lakes was the WILLIAM P. FESSENDEN, a 180-foot, side-wheel steamer which saw service from 1865-1908.

As mentioned earlier in this work, the FESSENDEN was built by Peck and Kirby in Cleveland, Ohio under the direct supervision of Captain Gilbert Knapp. For a period, here, the vessel's history becomes somewhat obfuscated. Originally, two side-wheel steamers were to be built, the FESSENDEN and the JOHN SHERMAN. Which one actually went into service is unclear. Mansfield's *History of the Great Lakes* speaks of a speed trial from Cleveland to Detroit between FESSENDEN and the COMMODORE PERRY in 1866 after which the FESSENDEN and JOHN SHERMAN exchanged names at Detroit. Most biographers of Captain Knapp tend to support this. Unfortunately, the *Record of Movements* contains no record for the COMMODORE PERRY between November

13, 1865 when she was ordered to Erie and November 16, 1872 when she was ordered into winter quarters. Although PERRY'S regular station was Erie, it is not beyond the realm of possibilities that she could indeed have engaged in a race to Detroit with the FESSENDEN. The entry for the SHERMAN sheds no further light on the mystery listing only two facts: that there was no record of acquisition and that it was sold June 25, 1872. The listings for the FESSENDEN serve only to further the confusion with these entries:

"1866, May 23—Ordered to Detroit for duty.

1866, June 22—The above order revoked, and ordered to have name changed to SHERMAN.

1866, July 2—Ordered revoked and name not changed."

Whichever cutter she really was, FESSENDEN saw duty in the Cleveland area until May 15, 1882 when she was turned over to the Union Dry Dock Company for rebuilding. Her old hull was sold and she was refitted with an iron hull.

Typical revenue cutter crew, circa 1890.

On April 26, 1883 she was successfully re-launched and returned to active service around Cleveland until 1885 when her cruising grounds were changed to extend from the mouth of the Detroit River through Lakes St. Clair and Huron to the Straits of Mackinac. At times during her career, FESSENDEN's cruises would extend from the Niagara River through all five of the Great Lakes. She was apparently quite a popular public attraction and participated in numerous community events, most notably the unveiling of Logan Monument in Chicago July 22, 1897, the Grand Army of the Republic (GAR) National Encampment at Buffalo, August 23, 1897, the Milwaukee Carnival Week each year between 1898 and 1901 and the celebration of Commodore Perry's victory at Cleveland September 10, 1901. In 1903 she left the Lakes and would not return until 1908 when she was decommissioned and sold to the Craig Shipbuilding Company of Toledo, Ohio for $9,100.00.

Other cutters on the Lakes included the MORRILL, which served off the southeastern coast until 1898 when ordered to Milwaukee. One of the MORRILL's duties while on the Lakes was to patrol regattas, a task she performed quite efficiently beginning with the T. J. Lipton Cup in 1905 and followed by the U.S. Military Tournament, Detroit, 1909, Oswegatchie Yacht Club, Ogdensburg, New York, 1912, Inter-Lake Yachting Association, Put-In-Bay, 1912, Buffalo Motor Boat Club, 1912 and numerous others. She also participated in the Livingston Channel Opening, October 19, 1912 and the July 4, 1913 Put-In-Bay Centennial Celebration. During World War I she was transferred to the Navy and saw duty on the New England Coast until February 14, 1918 when she returned to Detroit where she remained until 1925 when she left the Lakes for assignment to the Eastern Division. She was sold in 1928.

Also on the Lakes were the GEORGE M. BIBB, from 1882 to 1890; the MANHATTAN (later ARUNDEL), from 1875 to 1883; the CALUMET, from 1894 to 1898; the SALMON P. CHASE, 1865 to 1875; the DALLAS, 1903 to 1908; the ANDREW JOHNSON, 1865 to 1897; the JOHN A. DIX, 1865 to 1872; the MACKINAC, 1903-1917; and the TUSCARORA, 1902 to 1930.

For the most part the cutters were engaged in enforcing the customs laws, providing logistic support to the outlying U. S. Life Saving Service Stations and after 1871 assistance to distressed mariners. As we shall see in the succeeding chapters, the Revenue Cutter Service merged with the Life Saving Service in 1915 to form the nucleus of today's U. S. Coast Guard.

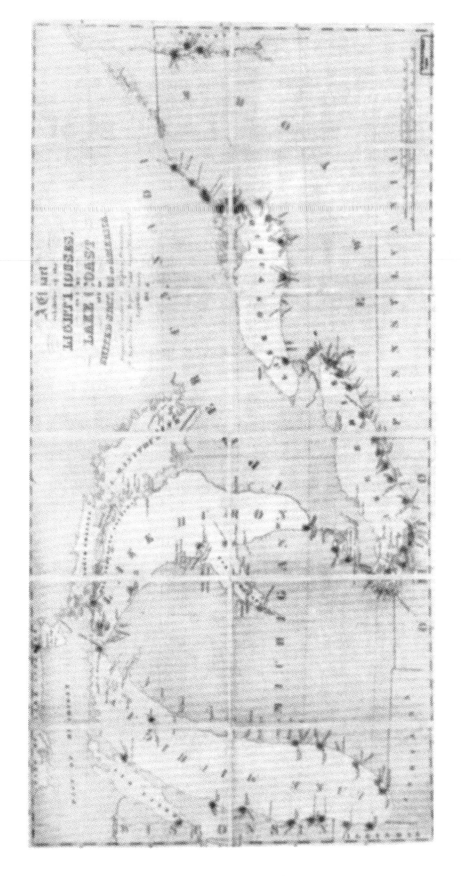

Chart exhibiting lighthouses on the Lake Coasts of the U. S. of America, prepared by order of Stephen Pleasanton, Fifth Auditor of the Treasury, and Superintendent General of Lighthouses.

1789 *Lighthouse Service* 1939

CHAPTER II
THE LIGHTHOUSE SERVICE

The use of lights to mark the coastline is almost as old as maritime commerce itself and indeed the development of a nation's lighthouse system can be seen to parallel the growth and development of its waterborne trade. In our own country, this pattern can readily be seen, for as early as 1716, sixty years before the Declaration of Independence, the first American lighthouse was established on Little Brewster Island at the entrance to Boston Harbor. In all, there were twelve lighthouses in existence when the first U. S. Congress met in 1789. Recognizing the importance of lighthouses to their fledgling nation's maritime commerce, the ninth law passed by that first Congress, created the Lighthouse Establishment as a unit of the Federal Government and delegated to the Secretary of the Treasury the authority and responsibility for "the necessary support, maintenance and repairs of all lighthouses, beacons, buoys and public piers erected, placed, or sunk before the passing of this act, at the entrance of, or within any bay, inlet, harbor, or port of the United States, for rendering the navigation thereof easy and safe...".

During the early period of the Lighthouse Establishment, superintendence of lighthouse matters alternated between the Secretary of the Treasury (1789-1792 and again from 1802-1813) and the Commissioner of the Revenue (1792-1802 and 1813-1820). A certain stability in the superintendence of the lighthouses was achieved in 1820 when Stephen Pleasonton, the Fifth Auditor of the Treasury, assumed these duties and carried them out for nearly thirty-three years.

Controversy has long existed over which light was the first to operate on the Great Lakes, Presq'isle (later changed to Presque Isle), or Buffalo. Records are not specific, so many were destroyed by a fire in the Treasury Department in 1920 that tracing the history of these two lights through official documents, is difficult, at best, and those records available add only confusion to the problem.

Joseph Torbett, in a paper on the Presque Isle Lighthouse published by the Public Information Division of the U. S. Coast Guard, declares that it was preceded in 1813 by the

Original Act creating the U. S. Lighthouse Service.

13

Niagara Fort Light on Lake Ontario. The *List of Lighthouses, Lighted Beacons, and Floating Lights* issued in 1866 would seem to bear this out, for it lists Niagara Fort Light and gives 1813 as the date of building. Congress, however, makes no mention of the Niagara Fort Light until May 7, 1822 when it appropriated one thousand dollars "for placing a lamp on the mess-house at Fort Niagara."

Erie's light, on the other hand, is more readily documented, for on May 1, 1810 Congress passed an act authorizing the Secretary of the Treasury to establish "such lights as he shall deem proper on or near Bird Island, and on or near Presq'isle, in Lake Erie. Apparently on the very same day, John Kelso, of Erie, gave two acres of land for a lighthouse. One thousand six hundred dollars were allocated in the act for the two lights and, in 1811, an additional four thousand dollars was provided. On March 13, 1812 the State of Pennsylvania ceded the two acres of land to the Federal Government, but the War of 1812 presumably delayed the building of a structure, for each year until 1817, Congress carried forward all but ten dollars of those first two appropriations. March 3, 1817 seventeen thousand dollars was appropriated for the two Lake Erie lighthouses and in 1818, the Presque Isle Light was completed. Faded and flame-marked records in the National Archives indicate this to be true as that is the date given by the Superintendent of the Lighthouse Establishment in his report to the Secretary of the Navy, dated December 1, 1839. Some doubt exists as to what happened to the original 1818 light, but it is generally accepted that the round stone tower now known as the "Old Land Lighthouse" and a part of a park at the entrance to Erie Bay, is the original light.

April 4, 1811, the State of New York ceded "a piece of land for a lighthouse in Buffalo, Niagara county." Early in 1817 Oliver Forward, as collector of the port, was commissioned to buy a site and for $350 he obtained the low, sandy point at the confluence of Buffalo Creek and Lake Erie.

The structure there was completed in 1820 and although there was as yet no harbor, Forward considered the light of such importance that, on his own responsibility, he appointed a temporary keeper to serve until official action was taken in Washington. The light was a stone tower, thirty feet in height, but smoke from nearby industry rendered it useless to mariners

and in 1833 a new light was erected.

Buffalo Historic Light (Photo by Gordon S. Smith)

Following the construction of these first lights, establishment of other stations moved into full swing as Congress authorized "a lighthouse on Galloo Island, near the outlet of Lake Ontario, . . . at or between the mouth of Grand River, in the State of Ohio, and the mouth of Detroit River, in the Territory of Michigan" on March 3, 1819 and "a lighthouse near Fort Gratiot, in Michigan Territory," in 1823. The latter was completed August 8, 1825 with Rufus Hatch being named keeper. George McDougall became the second keeper six weeks later when Hatch died. The early light had its share of problems for in addition to being located too far south so that pilots could not see the light until near the mouth of the St. Clair River, it also had defects in the foundation. These caused cracks in the walls and in 1828, the light began to lean. A three day storm that September pounded the structure with wind and waves of such force that the foundation was undermined and in November, it collapsed.

Congress appropriated $8,000 on March 2, 1829 for a new tower and in April Lucius Lyon was awarded the contract. The structure was 74 feet high and 25 feet in diameter, constructed of brick and completed in December of 1829. In 1861, the height was increased to 86 feet and in 1874 a brick duplex was added for the keeper and his assistants. The structure still stands today. McDougall remained keeper until 1842 when William Church took over.

May 23, 1828 Congress granted $5,000 for the construction of a lighthouse at Portland, New York on the shore of Lake Erie. Originally, the light apparatus was to consist of eleven patent lamps with fourteen inch reflectors, supplied by double tin oil butts capable of holding 500 gallons of oil. However, in the nearby village of Fredonia, there lived an ingenious gunsmith, W. A. Hart, who had harnessed a fountain of natural gas which he conveyed to the village's shops and taverns where it was used in place of the oil lamps. Upon completion of the light in 1829, a group was gathered in an effort to supply this gas to the new structure. They first dug a well, forty or fifty feet in diameter and about three feet deep over which a cone of solid masonry was placed to contain the gas. A pipe was inserted at the cone's base, bent toward the well bottom and then along the brook bed to its termination below the dam. The gas then travelled the final 230 rods to the lighthouse through underground pipes.

Since the concept of burning natural gas in a lighthouse was entirely new, Mr. Hart had to invent and construct a stand of lamps capable of receiving, emitting, and burning the gas. These lamps were arranged in two tiers with seven on the bottom and six above, so interspaced that the light gave the appearance of a single constant blaze when viewed from the lake. The new light did not, however, completely replace the oil lamp, for there were many problems and often oil had to be used instead. The Portland Harbor Light itself was discontinued in 1859, less than thirty years after it was first lit.

By 1838, the Lighthouse Service, like the country, was expanding rapidly. In order to have the system of aids to navigation surveyed and evaluated, Congress authorized the President to divide the service into eight districts. Two of these districts were along the Great Lakes. A Navy officer was detailed to each district to inspect the lights and the task of reporting on the Lakes, west of Detroit, fell to Lieutenant James T. Homans who would travel more than 1,800 miles on his tour of those early lights.

Leaving Detroit July 20, 1838, Homans travelled ". . . through Detroit river, lake and river St. Clair, Lake Huron, Saginaw Bay, Straits of Michilimackinac, east and west side of Lake Michigan to Green bay, . . . St. Mary's river, . . . Sault Ste. Marie . . ." and Mackinaw. Homans found the lights in his district to be in pretty good shape for the shape they were in. For example, in commenting on the light on Thunder Bay Island he warns, "the buildings are in danger of washing away, the house requires considerable repairs and the plaster is falling off;" then adds "It was, in other respects, . . . in good order". Bois Blanc Light, on the other hand, had already been washed away by gales and a new site selected, somewhat further back from the lake shore and on much higher ground.

Satisfied with this choice, Homans moved on to St. Joseph, Michigan City, Chicago and Saginaw before he reached the Straits of Michilimackinac and the Lakes' first Lightship. Stationed at the junction of Lakes Huron and Michigan, this early lightship was ill-suited for its task and often spent more time off station than on. At the time Lt. Homans arrived, the vessel was undergoing extensive repairs, having been driven ashore during a heavy gale. Mechanics and materials were hard to come by in Mackinaw and most supplies had to be ordered from Detroit, so there was great delay in returning the ship to her station. No sooner had she returned to duty when again she was driven from her place by heavy seas and wind. In his report, the Lieutenant suggested the lightship be moved to Lake St. Clair and a replacement built immediately.

The situation could have been alleviated, Homans reported, by the erection of a lighthouse on "Wagooshance shoal". Appropriations had already been set aside for the construction of this light and estimates called for completion in two years. By 1843, however, the ship was still in use and, in a report to the Secretary of the Treasury, Wm. Duane Wilson, General Inspector of Lights on the Northwestern Lakes, described it as ". . . a lightship of inferior construction, and very unfit for the objects intended—being unable, in stormy seasons, to keep her moorings . . .". Wilson, again, called for construction of a fixed light but it would not be until eight years later, in 1851, that the Waugoshance Lighthouse was opened and the lightship decommissioned.

The year 1851 proved an important one for the Lighthouse Establishment, as Congress directed that from time to time, Army engineer officers be detailed to superintend the construction and renovation of lighthouses. This legislation also contained a provision directing the Secretary of the Treasury to appoint a board, whose duty it would be to make a detailed report and program to guide legislators in their efforts to extend and improve the system of construction, illumination, inspection and superintendence of the Lighthouse Establishment. The board was to be made up of two high-ranking naval officers, two Army engineers, a civilian scientist and a junior naval officer to act as secretary.

Accordingly, on May 21, 1851, a board was appointed. After making a thorough study of the Service's work and administration and comparing conditions with those of Great Britain and France, the board reached the conclusion that our system was far inferior to those of Europe and recommended complete reorganization including appointment of a permanent board to supervise the Service.

The report, filed January 30, 1852, was disputed by Stephen Pleasonton, Fifth Auditor and Superintendent of the Lighthouse Establishment, who urged the appointment of a single officer, with full power and responsibility, under the Secretary of the Treasury. Creation of such a post, Pleasonton felt, would provide the most efficient and economical administration.

Accepting the Board's recommendation, however, Congress, on August 31, 1852, passed legislation recognizing the Lighthouse Board, whose members would be Presidential appointees. In addition to the original members, Congress added a second scientist, an Army engineer to act as co-secretary and defined the type of Army engineers required as one

engineer and one topographical engineer. This original Board consisted of: Admiral W. B. Shubrick, USN; Commander S. F. Dupont, USN; Brevet Brigadier General Joseph G. Totten, Corps of Engineers; Lieutenant Colonel James Kearney, Corps of Topographical Engineers; Professor Alexander D. Bache, Superintendent, U. S. Coast Survey and Professor Joseph Henry of the Smithsonian Institute with Lieutenant Thornton S. Jenkins, USN; and Captain Edmund L. F. Hardcastle, Corps of Topographical Engineers as co-secretaries. Committees were formed to administrate the various activities of the Service; finance, engineering, lighting, etc., and Admiral Shubrick was selected as the first chairman of the Lighthouse Board.

The Board's first duty was to reorganize the Service into districts, not to exceed twelve in number, each district to be assigned a lighthouse inspector subject to the orders of the Lighthouse Board. Under this reapportionment, the Great Lakes became the Tenth and Eleventh Districts.

Lighthouse construction on the Lake coasts flourished with the rising maritime commerce of the area. By 1865 there were seven lights on Lake Ontario; twelve on Lake Erie; two on Lake St. Clair; ten on Lake Huron; twenty-six on Lake Michigan and fifteen on Lake Superior. These lights, as reported in the *List of Lighthouses and Lighted Beacons of the Coasts of the Northern and Northwestern Lakes of the United States* compiled by the secretaries of the Lighthouse Board and dated January 1, 1866, were:

Lake Ontario: Galloo Island, established 1820, refitted 1857

Horse Island, established 1831, refitted 1857 (light on keeper's dwelling)

Stoney Point, established 1837, refitted 1857 (light on keeper's dwelling)

Oswego, established 1837, refitted 1857

Big Sodus Bay, established 1825, refitted 1859

Genesee, established 1822, rebuilt 1858

Niagara Fort, established 1823, refitted 1857 (light on messhouse—Fort built 1813)

Lake Erie: Horse-shoe Reef, established 1856
Buffalo, established 1828, refitted 1857 (replaced original light est. 1820)

Old Cleveland Light 1873-1893

Dunkirk, established 1837, rebuilt 1857

Presque Isle, established 1838, rebuilt 1858 (replaced original light est. 1818)

Grand River (Fairport), established 1828, rebuilt 1858

Cleveland, established 1829, refitted 1859 (lighted with gas)

Black River, established 1836, rebuilt 1857

Sandusky, established 1831, rebuilt 1858

Port Clinton, established 1832, refitted 1864

Green Island, established 1854

West Sister Island, established 1847, refitted 1857

Turtle Island, established 1831, refitted 1857

Monroe, established 1849, refitted 1855

Lake St. Clair: St. Clair Flats, established 1859

Windmill Point, established 1838, refitted 1865

Lake Huron: Fort Gratiot, established 1825, refitted 1862

Point Aux Barques, established 1847, rebuilt 1857

Ottawa (Tawas) Point, established 1853, refitted 1856

Charity Island, established 1857

Saginaw Bay, established 1841, refitted 1863

Thunder Bay Island, established 1832, refitted 1857

Presque Isle, established 1840, refitted 1857

Bois Blanc, established 1839, refitted 1857, (replaced earlier light —washed away)

Cheboygan, established 1851, rebuilt 1859 (light on keeper's dwelling)

Detour, established 1847, rebuilt 1861

Lake Michigan: Waugoshance, established 1851, (replaced lightship)

Skilligallee (Ile aux Galets), established 1850, refitted 1857 (light on keeper's dwelling)

Beaver Island Harbor, established 1856

Beaver Island, established 1851, rebuilt 1858

Grand Traverse, established 1852, rebuilt 1858 (light on keeper's dwelling)

South Manitou, established 1839, rebuilt 1858 (light on keeper's dwelling)

Point Betsey (Point aux BecScies), established 1858

Muskegon, established 1851, refitted 1856 (light on keeper's dwelling)

Grand River, established 1855

Kalamazoo, established 1852, rebuilt 1859 (light on keeper's dwelling)

St. Joseph's, established 1831, rebuilt 1859 (light on keeper's dwelling)

Michigan City, established 1837, rebuilt 1858 (light on keeper's dwelling)

Chicago, established 1859 (replaced earlier light established in 1832)

Waukegan, established 1849, rebuilt 1860 (light on keeper's dwelling)

Kenosha, established 1848, rebuilt 1858

Racine, established 1829, rebuilt 1858

Milwaukee, established 1855

Port Washington, established 1849, rebuilt 1860 (light on keeper's dwelling)

Sheboygan, established 1839, rebuilt 1860 (light on keeper's dwelling)

Manitowoc, established 1839, refitted 1859

St. Joseph Lighthouse

Ontonagon, established 1852, refitted 1857 (light on keeper's
dwelling)
La Pointe, established 1858, (light
on keeper's dwelling)
Raspberry Island, established 1862,
(light on keeper's dwelling)
Minnesota Point, established 1857

Between 1852 and 1859 practically all lighthouses of the United States, including those on
the Great Lakes, were refitted with lenticular
apparatus (Fresnel lens) replacing the earlier
Argand lamps and parabolic reflectors. The
Fresnel lens was comprised of a powerful central lamp which emitted luminous beams in all
directions and around which glass was arranged in such a way as to refract those beams
into parallel rays aimed in the desired direction.

Third Order Fresnel Lens

Bayley's Harbor, established 1852,
refitted 1858
Port de Moris, established 1849, rebuilt 1858 (light on keeper's
dwelling)
Pottawatomie, established 1858, rebuilt 1858 (replaced earlier light,
washed away)
Point Peninsula, established 1865
Green Island, established 1863
(light on keeper's dwelling)
Tail Point, established 1848, rebuilt
1859 (light on keeper's dwelling)

Lake Superior: Round Island, established 1855, refitted 1864 (light on keeper's
dwelling)
Point Iroquois, established 1857
White Fish Point, established 1847,
rebuilt 1861
Grand Island, established 1856
Marquette, established 1853, refitted 1856
Portage River, established 1856
Manitou, established 1849, rebuilt
1861
Copper Harbor, established 1848,
refitted 1859
Eagle Harbor, established 1850, refitted 1857, (light on keeper's
dwelling)
Eagle River, established 1858, (light
on keeper's dwelling)

18

Fresnel classified these lenses into orders ranging from one to six. The numbers indicated the magnitude and intensity of the light. A first order lens stood nearly twelve feet high and six feet in diameter and cost between $4,500 and $8,000 while a sixth order lens measured only eleven and three-fourths inches in diameter and cost up to $315. Although initially quite expensive, within a few years, the Fresnel lens more than paid for itself as it reduced fuel costs to one-fourth of what had previously been required and increased the intensity of the light almost four times.

In addition to increasing the efficiency of the lights by employing the Fresnel lens, the Board also sought to increase economy by experimenting with various fuels. Sperm oil, which had been the mainstay of the Service, by 1862 had risen in price to $1.64½ per gallon. The Board commissioned some noted scientists to analyze sperm, whale, shark, fish, seal, colza, olive, lard and mineral oils in search of a cheaper fuel. Colza oil, which is derived mainly from wild cabbage seeds, had all the necessary properties of an inexpensive fuel source except that it had to be imported. To overcome this obstacle, the board began promoting the domestic production of this plant and the manufacture of its oil, purchasing 12,000 gallons in 1862 at a cost of $13,000, a savings of over $6,700 for a comparable amount of sperm oil.

From 1864 to 1867 lard oil became the standard illuminant, replacing both the colza and sperm oils. Despite this standard use of lard oil, experiments continued with other types of fuels. In 1864, a Lake Michigan lighthouse keeper, experimenting on his own, substituted a kerosene lamp for the regular lard oil one. A short time after lighting the lamp, he attempted to extinguish the flame by blowing down the chimney. Instead of going out, the lamp exploded, setting his clothes afire. He hurriedly descended the staircase and upon reaching the bottom, a second explosion blew the entire lantern from the tower, completely destroying the lenticular apparatus. Years of experiment later, mineral oil lamps would illuminate almost all the Service's lights.

On the 20th of May 1870, one of the most ambitious projects undertaken by the Lighthouse Board, began in Scammon's Harbor, Michigan. This site had been selected as the depot for construction of Spectacle Reef Light, a structure which would be erected on a dangerous shoal in Lake Huron, ten miles away from Bois Blanc Island, the nearest land, and seventeen miles from the depot. Because there were many special engineering problems associated with the light, Major O. M. Poe of the Army Corps of Engineers and a member of the Lighthouse Board was charged with the planning and construction of the light. One of the major engineering obstacles which had to be overcome involved the formation of ice-fields, which, pushed along by currents of three miles an hour often spread over an area of thousands of acres at a thickness of two feet, creating an almost irresistible force. Thus, the structure would have to be of such construction that the ice would be crushed and its motion so impeded as to cause its grounding on the shoal, forming a barrier against future floes.

To overcome the difficulties involved in the preparation of the foundation, a pier of protection, ninety-two feet square with a central opening of forty-eight square feet was constructed. After four temporary cribs had been placed, forming the bottom of the pier, a fleet was assembled to begin the final positioning. At eight P.M. on July 18, 1871, the tugs *Magnet* and *Champion* started towing the immense crib to the reef, followed by the lighthouse tenders WARRINGTON and BELLE, the tugs *Hand* and *Stranger*, barges *Ritchie* and *Emerald*, two scows of the Service and a workforce of 140 men. Six hours later, they arrived at the reef but had to await daylight before attempting to position the crib. With considerable difficulty, the crib was positioned and by four o'clock, all but 600 of the 1,800 tons of ballast-stone had been thrown into the compartments. By September 12th, the pier had reached its full height and workmen's quarters were completed by the 20th. Work then commenced on the coffer-dam and continued until the end of October when the onset of winter forced the curtailment of all activities.

Work on the tower did not resume until May 20th, although activity at the harbor began anew on May 3. It had been a severe winter and as late as May 13th, there remained several feet of ice in the coffer-dam with the pier of protection covered by ice masses, which had to be cleared before actual contruction could begin.

The stones used were all cut at the Scammon's Harbor depot and were formed so as to be interlocking. They were fitted together in courses, with the lower course bolted to the rock with three-foot long, wrought-iron bolts penetrating twenty-one inches into the rock. For the first thirty-four feet, the tower is solid stone. Each course of this section is bolted to the other by two-foot long bolts penetrating nine inches into the course below it. The bolts were all wedged at each end and the holes filled with pure Portland cement mortar. By the end of August, the entire solid portion of the tower had been set.

An unusually severe gale arose on the 28th of September causing considerable damage. Some idea of the ferociousness of this storm is provided by the superintendent of construction:

> The sea burst in the doors and windows of the workmen's quarters, tore up the floors and all bunks on the side nearest the edge of the pier, carried off the walk between the privy and pier, and the privy itself, and tore up the platform between the quarters and the pier. EVERYTHING in the quarters was completely demolished, except the kitchen, . . . the temporary cribs were completely swept away . . .

> A stone weighing over thirty pounds was thrown across the pier, a distance of 70 feet; but the greatest feat accomplished by the gale was the moving of the revolving derrick from the northeast to the southwest corner. At 3 o'clock in the morning the men were obliged to run for their lives, . . .

Spectacle Reef Light

A new site, chosen as the most sheltered, was secured for the crew's quarters. The temporary cribs had been carried away but since it was so late in the season, there was no time to replace the protective sheathing. Thus, the cribs which were used as boiler and coal rooms were filled with stone to provide some protection. Leaving two men to man the temporary light erected on the pier, the crew returned to Detroit on October 31st.

The workmen, returning to the reef with a special crane for setting the upper courses, were delayed by the late opening of the Straits of Mackinac and did not arrive until May 8, 1873. Again, ice had to be cleared from the pier before work could be begun. What had remained of the original workmen's quarters and the temporary light had been carried away by ice and totally destroyed. The light was replaced by an ordinary hand lantern until a new tower could be erected. By June, the first fifty feet of the tower's masonry had been completed. Work moved along steadily through the summer and at the end of September, all the stone was set up to and including the main deck and the interior brick work, except the arches between the beams of the three upper floors, was completed. Despite some unusually bad weather during September and October, the station was, for the most part, complete by October 31, 1873.

So severe was the winter of 1873-74 that the workmen were unable to return to Spectacle Reef until May 14th. They were greeted by a practical demonstration of the strength of the tower they had constructed, for the fierce winter had piled ice against the structure to a height of thirty feet. This was seven feet higher than the doorway and they could not enter the tower to complete their work until the iceberg had been cut away.

On the first of June 1874, the light was exhibited for the first time. It had taken over twenty months of actual working time (since no work could be done during the winter) and $406,000 to complete, but the Spectacle Reef Lighthouse, rising eighty-six feet three inches above the surface of Lake Huron is considered the finest specimen of monolithic stone masonry in the United States.

During the same period that Spectacle Reef Light was being constructed, plans were already being made for the erection of a similar offshore structure on Stannard Rock in Lake

Superior. The rapid increase of commerce between Duluth and the lower lakes necessitated such a light for, as stated by Brevet Major General G. Weitzel in his annual report of 1874, "The rock lies near the track of all the vessels turning to the northside and western portions of Lake Superior, and is an object of great concern and terror, especially in dark nights and the almost interminable fog which prevails . . ." General Weitzel recommended commencement of construction immediately, since the expensive and especially designed equipment used at Spectacle Reef were now available, but it was not until four years later, in 1877, that Congress appropriated $50,000 for the project and work actually began.

Although the engineering problems were similar to those at Spectacle Reef, Stannard Rock's were a bit more complex, compounded by its location, twenty-three miles from the nearest land and almost fifty miles from the closest harbor. Huron Bay was chosen as the site for a depot with all the construction machinery moved there from Scammon's Harbor. On June 18, 1877, workmen began clearing the grounds and erecting the eight buildings which had been transported in sections from Scammon's Harbor. A week later piles were driven for the wharf and on July 10th, the depot received its first cargo of timber.

When the protecting pier had been built up to a depth of four feet, it was towed out to the rock by the Lighthouse Steamer WARRINGTON, arriving August 24th. Once there, sixteen carpenters labored for four hours taking nearly a thousand soundings in order that the pier could be shimmed to conform to the contour of the rock. This completed, the crib was returned to the depot where it was planked on the bottom, shimmed and built up to a height of nine feet. Meanwhile, a party of carpenters, quarrymen and laborers was detailed to Huron Island where they opened a quarry, from which they supplied the ballast stone and concrete for the lighthouse. On October 23rd work was secured until spring.

Activity resumed May 14, 1878 and by August 4th, the protecting pier had been built up to thirteen feet above the bottom planking. It was then decked over into four water-tight compartments and filled with 875 tons of ballast stone. The steamers WARRINGTON and IRA CHAFFEE assisted by the tug *Dudley*, then began the fifty mile trek to Stannard Rock.

Arriving the next day, the pier was sunk in place but it was discovered that the water was one foot eight inches lower than the previous year and thus too shallow for the WARRINGTON to come alongside. The decision was made to move the pier to a spot sixty feet south and thirty feet west of the original site, rotating the structure 80° to compensate for the rock's uneven surface. Timber was added to the superstructure to correct any remaining inequities and by October, ten courses of timber had been added and filled with 4,926 tons of ballast rock. The pier was again decked over and all work closed for the season on October 26th.

Most of 1879 and 1880 were spent in constructing the permanent pier of iron and concrete. When finished, the pier rose twenty-three feet above water and thirty-five feet above the bedrock, measured sixty-two feet in diameter at the top, sixty-two feet five inches at the bottom and contained 7,246 tons of concrete. Having completed the pier and not having enough stone ready to commence work on the tower, work was closed August 22, 1880.

From July 4th to August 31st, 1881 work progressed steadily and all thirty-three courses of stone for the tower were set into place. Then, while awaiting the much delayed iron-work, a small party was employed in preparing the inside of the tower.

That winter, ice built up around the tower, extending eighteen feet above the top of the permanent pier. Fifteen men worked from May 24 to June 1st, 1882 to clear away the ice. The remaining work was completed during June and the lamp was exhibited for the first time on July 4, 1882.

The tower, 102 feet above Lake Superior cost $305,000 to complete and is considered a major engineering feat. It had taken five years to build, but that figure barely tells of the difficulties encountered. For instance, during the first sixty-nine days of work at the reef, forty-two were lost because the party was unable to land or was driven away by heavy weather. Whole cargoes of stone and much material also were lost during gales and other storms. The difficulties did not end when the tower was finished though. Because of its remote location and the often treacherous sea conditions, it became known as the "loneliest place in America", with some keepers spending an entire season stranded on the light.

In addition to tending their lights, keepers

often were called upon to render assistance to distressed mariners. Sometimes this aid had to come, not from the keepers, but from members of their families. One such case involved Miss Maebelle L. Mason, fourteen-year-old daughter of Captain Orlo Mason, keeper of the Mamajuda Lighthouse on the Detroit River. The

Detroit River Light

incident took place May 11, 1890 and began when a man in a rowboat attempted to secure a tow from the steamer *C. W. Elphicke*. His line missed connecting but caught in such a way as to capsize his small boat. Unable to assist the man, Captain Montague of the *Elphicke* signalled the keeper for help. Unfortunately, the keeper and his boat were away at the time, leaving the rescue up to his wife and daughter. A small punt being the only craft available, the two hurriedly set about launching it. Maebelle undertook the dangerous task of rowing out to the drowning man—a distance of about a mile. After a hearty effort, she came alongside the nearly exhausted man and succeeded in pulling him aboard. She then rowed back to the lighthouse with the submerged boat in tow. For her exceptional courage and human-

ity, the young lady received the Silver Lifesaving Medal. It was presented to her April 15, 1891 during the Grand Army of the Republic National Convention in Detroit. She was also awarded a Gold Medal with Maltese Cross from the Ship Masters Association.

The task of supplying and maintaining the lighthouses and other navigational aids of the Lighthouse Establishment was the responsibility of a small fleet of vessels operated by the Service. Prior to 1856, these "lighthouse tenders" were actually vessels chartered by the government and used primarily for constructing or repairing the early lights. Revenue cutters also were used for this purpose.

In 1856, two schooners, the CHALLENGE and the SKYLARK were purchased by the Lighthouse Board for use as supply vessels and lighthouse tenders. The two schooners were renamed on April 29, 1857, receiving the more appropriate names of LAMPLIGHTER and WATCHFUL. Both vessels served the Tenth Lighthouse District. LAMPLIGHTER was replaced in May 1862 by the chartered schooner DREAM, while the WATCHFUL remained in service until October 1867 when she was sold at public auction.

The eighty-eight foot schooner BELLE was the last sailing vessel operated by the Lighthouse Board as a tender. She was purchased in 1863 and assigned to the Eleventh Lighthouse District. BELLE, as seen earlier, was used quite extensively in the construction of Spectacle Reef Lighthouse, devoting full-time service to that project after the arrival of the Lakes' first steam-powered tender. The aging BELLE ran aground in the fall of 1873, sustaining such extensive damage that the Board ordered her sold on July 10, 1874.

On June 6, 1867, the Lighthouse Board purchased the HAZE, a steam-powered propeller, for $27,000. 124 feet overall, she had a twenty-three foot beam, and a single expansion steam engine rated at 292 horsepower. HAZE saw duty on all the Great Lakes, from the St. Lawrence River to the far reaches of Lake Superior, ferrying supplies, carrying the inspectors about on their tours and taking part in the construction and repair of lighthouses. The hard work she performed took its toll and in 1876, the fifteen-year-old vessel was practically rebuilt and given new engines. The work cost $29,606.75 but, so revitalized the tender as to enable her to continue in service until

March 15, 1905.

During construction of the Spectacle Reef Light, the need for a steam tender to augment the efforts of the schooner BELLE became apparent and thus the Lighthouse Board purchased the WARRINGTON, a single-screw, 152 foot, wooden-hulled vessel with a 400 horsepower steam engine. The WARRINGTON proved a workhorse during the construction of both Spectacle Reef and Stannard Rock Lighthouses and saw service in the Eleventh Lighthouse District until 1911 when she was phased out.

Lighthouse Tender HYACINTH

DAHLIA, a 141 foot, propeller steamer, has the distinction of being the first in several categories. Built in 1874 in Philadelphia, she

Lighthouse Tender SUMAC

was the first tender built especially for Great Lakes service, the first iron-hulled tender on the Lakes and the first on the Lakes to receive a botanical name. After 1865, it was the custom

of the U. S. Lighthouse Establishment to name tenders after flowers, trees, or plants and DAHLIA was the first new tender on the lakes to be so named. She served in the Eleventh Lighthouse District until 1886 when that district was reorganized to form the Ninth and Eleventh Districts. Finishing her thirty-five year career on Lake Michigan (Ninth District), she was sold for $5,400 on February 17, 1909.

Other tenders seeing service on the Great Lakes were: LOTUS (1880-1901), MARIGOLD (1890-1946) and AMARANTH (1891-1946).

Lighthouse Tender WALNUT

Tenders were not the only vessels employed by the Lighthouse Board, for, equally important, in the history of this Service, were those floating sentinels of navigation, the lightships. With the exception of the wooden vessel which preceded the Waugoshance Lighthouse from 1832-1851, there were no Federal lightships on the Great Lakes until 1891. In this year, the Craig Shipbuilding Company of Toledo, Ohio, built three wooden steam screw lightships for $42,675. Known officially as Lightships Nos. 55, 56, and 57, the three vessels were all 102 feet eight inches overall with illuminating apparatus consisting of two lanterns, one on the foremast and the other on the mainmast. The lanterns on Lightship No. 55 were a fixed red, while No. 56's were a fixed white and No. 57 had one white on the foremast and one red on the mainmast.

They were delivered to the Service at Detroit on September 14 and 15, 1891.

After being inspected and slightly modified, they left Detroit October 19, 1891. The DAHLIA took them in tow the next day and by the 24th they were all on station: No. 55 at Simmons

Reef, No. 56 at White Shoals and No. 57 at Gray's Reef.

Although Commander Nicoll Ludlow, USN, Ninth Lighthouse District Inspector, had been instructed to keep the light vessels on station until the close of the navigation season, the three ships, without orders, left for winter quarters between the 17th and 20th of November. Guarded by the DAHLIA, they were returned to their posts, where they remained until the close of the season.

According to the *Annual Report of the Lighthouse Service, 1892*, the officers and crew involved were discharged for dereliction of duty and replaced. The incident did serve to bring about much-needed reform and the following year the Secretary of the Treasury gave responsibility for appointing keepers and assistant keepers to the Board, taking it out of the hands of the Collectors of Customs.

The vessels served faithfully each year on their same stations until 1900, when, on July 10th, Lightship No. 55 was replaced on Simmons Reef by a gas buoy and she in turn replaced the gas buoy on Lansing Shoal (Lake Michigan).

Poe Reef Light

St. Clair Lightship

During 1907, the trio of Lightships were used to test the new submarine fog-bells. Found to be quite effective, these signals would remain on the lightships until their discontinuance.

September 1, 1910 White Shoals Lightship No. 56 was replaced by a lighthouse and she was transferred to North Manitou Shoal where she served until 1927 when she was transferred to Grays Reef. The following year she was sold for $1,100 to Henry Osby of Milwaukee, ending thirty-seven years of service.

Huron Lightship No. 61

In all, twenty different lightships saw service on the Great Lakes, manning eighteen different stations from 1891 to 1970. More information on some of these lightships is contained elsewhere in this narrative.

Lansing Shoals Light

Poe Reef Lightship

In the years following the erection of Spectacle Reef Lighthouse, changes affecting the Lighthouse Service began taking place at a rapid rate. In 1875, the first steam fog signal on Lake Michigan was installed at South Manitou Light. An Act of Congress on August 14th that same year provided for the prosecution of persons who "willfully and unlawfully" damaged any pier, breakwater or other government work done for the improvement of navigation and established punishment as "a fine not exceeding one thousand dollars."

Masters of lighthouse tenders were given "police powers in matters pertaining to government property and smuggling" by Act of Congress, June 16, 1880 and the duties of collectors of customs relating to lighthouses were transferred to the Lighthouse Board.

Requirements for providing lights on bridges over navigable waters were established by Congress in 1882. That same year, the Secretary of the Navy began a vigorous campaign to transfer the Lighthouse and Lifesaving Services and the Coast Survey to the Navy Department. In his annual reports from 1882 to 1885, he argued that the work of these Services were essentially naval in character and required the "kind of skill and experience that the Navy alone can furnish." His efforts, however, met with such stiff opposition from the Secretary of the Treasury and others involved, that he eventually gave up the fight.

Uniforms for male keepers, masters, mates and engineers of tenders were first introduced to the Service in 1884 to "aid in maintaining its discipline, increase its efficiency, raise its tone and add to its esprit de corps." By the following year, all 1,600 men of the Service had been outfitted and the wearing of both the dress and fatigue uniforms was made mandatory. Acting keepers were not permitted to wear the new uniform.

On July 26, 1886, Congress passed the *Reorganization Act* and effectually restructured the Service, with the Great Lakes being redivided into three districts. The Tenth District continued to encompass Lakes Ontario and Erie but the Eleventh was divided with the newly created Ninth District encompassing Lake Michigan and the Eleventh, Lakes Superior and Huron.

As we have shown, the Presidency of Andrew Jackson began the widespread employment of political favorites in Federal jobs. This so-called "spoils system" was to plague the administration of the Lighthouse Establishment throughout its early history, teaching a peak of infamy during the administration of U. S. Grant. Under Grant, the system flourished to such an extent that all levels of government became permeated with corruption and the Collectors of Customs, who, in effect, appointed keepers of lighthouses and lightships, were no exception.

The whole issue of the "spoils system" came to a head on July 2, 1881 when Charles J. Guiteau, a mentally unbalanced man who had unsuccessfully sought the consulship in Vienna, assassinated President James A. Garfield. However tragic this shooting of the President was, it served to shock the American people into an awareness of evils of the system. An outraged public demanded reform and in response on January 16, 1883, Congress passed the *Pendleton Civil Service Act*. President Chester A. Arthur, himself, a former Collector of Customs, was given the authority to decide which federal offices would be classified (positions for which examinations would have to be taken) and although the initial list contained only about ten percent of the total positions, it did include those applying to customhouses. Succeeding Presidents would continually broaden the list and in 1896, Grover Cleveland added the U. S. Lighthouse Service.

By 1900 the United States had transformed itself from an agrarian to an industrial nation with both foreign and domestic trade prospering. In an effort to keep pace with both an increasing commerce and an expanding labor force, the Department of Commerce and Labor was created by Act of Congress, July 1, 1903. The Lighthouse Board, Coast and Geodetic Survey and other agencies concerned with navigation were transferred to this new department.

During the next seven years, the board form of organization, under which the Lighthouse Service had operated since 1852, came under almost constant criticism from its new department. Both Oscar S. Straus who served as Secretary of the Department of Commerce and Labor from 1906-1909 and his successor, Charles Nagel argued vigorously that the Service had grown to such proportions that the Lighthouse Board could no longer effectively administer control. Two of their major criticisms were the lack of an executive head with definitive authority and responsibility and the friction caused by the division of authority in each district between the Naval inspector and Army engineer.

They effectively presented their case and on June 17, 1910, Congress dissolved the Lighthouse Board creating in its stead, the Bureau of Lighthouses. The Act (36 Stat. L., 534) provided for a Commissioner of Lighthouses, a Deputy Commissioner, a Chief Construction Engineer and a Superintendent of Naval Construction to be appointed by the President. July 1st President Taft named George R. Putnam as Commissioner and Arthur V. Conover as his Deputy Commissioner. These appointments were followed by the naming of John S. Conway as Chief Construction Engineer and George Warrington as Superintendent of Naval Construction in December. After a year and a half, Conway replaced Conover as Deputy and H. B. Bowerman was named Chief Construction Engineer, June 12, 1912. Warrington left the Service after about four years and was replaced by his Principal Assistant Engineer Edward C. Gillette. Following Gillette's appointment, the Commission achieved great stability for almost two decades as Putnam served on the Commission for twenty-five years; Conway, twenty; Bowerman, twenty-one and Gillette, twenty-eight.

The field administration of the Lighthouse Service, a major point in the Straus-Nagel reports, had also been restructured by the Act. Replacing the old division of authority between the Naval inspector and Army Engineer was a single official. The Lighthouse Inspector, as he was now called, had authority over all lighthouse work in his district, and was directly responsible to the Bureau for the performance of his duties. Lighthouse Inspectors were all civilians with the exception of the three river district inspectors who were officers of the Army Corps of Engineers.

Basically unaffected by the 1910 reorganization, the functions of the Lighthouse Service continued at an onerous pace throughout this period. Two notable lights were constructed on the Lakes during this time; Rock of Ages Light in the Northern portion of Lake Superior, west of Isle Royal, was completed in 1908. The station was so difficult to reach during the stormy season that one year, when the tender arrived at the close of navigation to pick up the four keepers, their only remaining food was a single can of tomatoes.

The second important structure was Split Rock Light, completed in 1910. This light, also on the northern shore of Lake Superior, is picturesquely located atop an imposing rock. The tower itself is 54 feet high but because of the added height of the rock, it rises 178 feet above lake level. Through the years it has become one of the most frequently visited lighthouses in the United States.

Split Rock Light

Life at a lighthouse was often both difficult and tedious. Keepers were required to maintain their lights in a constant state of readiness, keep their premises clean, grounds in order and do all painting and minor repairs themselves. To take some of the drudgery out of these unspectacular yet necessary duties, the Bureau of Lighthouses, in the summer of 1911 initiated a system of efficiency stars and pennants. This system, in addition to promoting friendly competition and increasing efficiency, also served to raise the morale of the Service.

During each quarter, the District Inspector would issue a circular listing the names of all keepers in his district who had been commended on the general efficiency and neatness of their station and personnel during the preceeding quarter. Those keepers receiving commendations at each quarterly inspection during the fiscal year were awarded the inspector's efficiency star, which they were entitled to wear during the next fiscal year. Keepers winning the star for three successive years were awarded the Commissioner's efficiency star.

Besides their aesthetic value, the stars held considerable importance in the selection of

Battle Island Light, Nipigon Bay, Lake Superior

Point Iroquois Light, Brimley, Michigan

Operation Lamplighter—This was the last view of the cutter WOODBINE for the crew of White Shoals Light Station until the ice again rims the station in the fall. Weekly supply runs are made from Charlevoix Lifeboat Station.

Keeper Alfred G. Bauman opens door of Maumee Bay Range Light.

Racine Reef Light

keepers for duty, promotion, etc. Precedence was given to those wearing the Commissioner's star, followed by those wearing the Inspector's star, then on order of efficiency as documented from official records and lastly on length of service.

The station receiving the highest marks for general efficiency during an entire fiscal year would receive the "efficiency pennant" and the names of the keepers were published both in a circular by the Inspector and the "Lighthouse Service Bulletin", a monthly publication begun in January 1912 and distributed to all personnel.

Late fall, 1913, for only the second time in the Service's history, a lightship foundered at her moorings. The first incident occurred on August 23, 1893 when the Five Fathom Bank, Lightship No. 37 was lost in the rough seas off the entrance to Delaware Bay. The second, November 10, 1913, involved Lightship No. 82 on Lake Erie, about thirteen miles southwest of Buffalo.

Navigation would normally be closed at this late date but 1913 had been an extremely good year, weather-wise, and there was still very little ice in evidence, so the Great Lakes Fleet had continued operating. Beginning November 10th, a severe storm swept across the Lakes. By the time it was over, twelve ships and more than 200 lives had been lost. Among those lost were Lightship No. 82, Hugh H. Williams, her Captain, Andrew Lehy, the mate, Charles Butler, Chief Engineer, Cornelius Lehy, his assistant, Peter Mackey, cook and Seaman William Jensen. Despite an intensive search, the Lightship was not located until the following season, about two miles from her station. In 1915 she was raised and refurbished, finishing out her career as a Relief Lightship and Lightship Tender.

Lightships and lighthouses were not the only aids to navigation operated by the Service. Beacons, buoys and fog signals, important elements in providing improved navigation also underwent extensive development during the

Service's first one hundred and twenty-five years.

The first fog signals appear to have been bells, rung by hand but by 1851 mechanically operated bells had been introduced and an air fog whistle operated by an air compressor had been experimented with. In 1855 steam whistles were investigated as possible fog signals followed by the introduction of sirens in 1868. The first steam fog signal on Lake Michigan was installed in 1875 at South Manitou Island Lighthouse.

About the same time that the early fog bells came into use, 1820, spar buoys began replacing the earlier barrel buoys. It was not until 1850 that there was any standard for numbering or coloring buoys. That year, Congress passed an Act (9 Stat. L., 500, 504) that provided for all buoys, which appeared on the right as approached from seaward, to be painted red and even-numbered. Those on the left were to be black and odd-numbered. Those marking shoals with a channel on either side were painted with red and black horizontal stripes and buoys in channel ways were colored with black and white perpendicular stripes.

By the turn of the century, most fog signals in use on the Great Lakes were steam whistles. Often, these whistles were difficult to operate. Because they received their power from steam, their use required building fires under boilers and it usually took forty-five minutes to an hour to get up enough steam to start the whistle working. Frequently, by the time the whistle began sounding, the fog had disappeared. These signals were later replaced by ones operated with compressed air supplied by internal combustion engines or motor-driven compressors.

Lighted buoys were not extensively utilized during the latter part of the nineteenth and early twentieth centuries because they could only be obtained from Germany and were quite expensive to operate. A gas called Pintsch gas, manufactured from oil, was used as fuel, hence they became known as Pintsch type buoys. The gas had to be pumped into the main body of the buoy to a pressure of 180 psi, requiring a lighthouse tender equipped with compressors, to pull alongside and pump the gas through a hose into the buoy. In 1910 a buoy using compressed acetylene gas was introduced and eventually replaced the Pintsch-type buoys.

In 1915, the Lighthouse Service installed temporary unwatched gas lights at certain isolated stations on the Great Lakes. Installed in late fall, these temporary lights permitted keepers to depart their stations under less hazardous circumstances while still providing guidance to mariners who continued to operate after the close of the regular season.

By 1918, electricity, telephones and radio beacons had come to the Lighthouse Service. An Act of Congress that year also provided retirement benefits for persons in the field, including keepers and lightship crews. The Lighthouse Service had come a long way in its first one hundred years on the Great Lakes.

CHAPTER III
THE LIFE SAVING SERVICE

Despite the numerous accomplishments and sometimes daring exploits of both the Revenue Cutter and Lighthouse Services, the real makers of history among the Coast Guard's predecessors were the men of the U. S. Life Saving Service.

A government-operated service did not arrive on the Lakes until 1876 but its roots, both nationally and regionally, originated as the concern of a few brave volunteers who sought to help preserve life by aiding mariners who wrecked along our coasts.

The pioneer organization was the Massachusetts Humane Society, formed in 1785, which erected the first American Lifeboat Station in 1807 at Cohasset. Other stations were established as funds permitted. They were equipped with lifeboats and manned by volunteer crews.

Government involvement in the field of lifesaving began in 1837 when an Act of Congress directed the Revenue Cutter Service to make "seasonal cruises along the coast for the relief of distressed mariners . . .". There was no provision in the Act for shore-based assistance but the following year, reporting on lighthouses, the Senate Committee on Commerce suggested that lifeboats be stationed at various lights to aid distressed mariners. This suggestion was reinforced by the publishers of *Blunt's Coast Pilot* and a report on Great Britain's Lighthouse system prepared for the Secretary of the Treasury in 1846 and presented to the 29th Congress.

It was a Representative from the Great Lakes state of Michigan, Robert McClelland, who introduced to Congress, a motion, which provided "For furnishing the lighthouses on the Atlantic Coast with means of rendering assistance to shipwrecked mariners, . . ." This addition to the Act of March 3, 1847 (9 Stat. L., 175, 176) was the first appropriation of federal monies for shore-based assistance to distressed mariners. The five thousand dollars appropriated went untouched for almost two years.

The fight for some form of lifesaving institution was renewed August 3, 1848 when William Newell, a New Jersey Congressman, incited by a series of wrecks along the coast of his state, made a highly emotional and enthusiastic appeal. The effective oratory induced his fellows to appropriate $10,000 for lifesaving equipment for the coastal area between Sandy Hook and Little Egg Harbor in the Act of August 14, 1848 (9 Stat. L., 321, 322).

Although well-intentioned, the Newell Act was next to meaningless for it merely provided money for the purchase of equipment. Nowhere in the Act was any mention made of how the equipment would be used or maintained or even who would use it. It did assign an officer of the Revenue Cutter Service to expend the funds but Captain Alexander V. Fraser, Chief of the Service, was neither given authority to spend the money nor provided any funds to work this appropriation into his existing administrative system.

Captain Douglass Ottinger of the Revenue Cutter Service, was appointed to oversee the expenditure of the money and he employed the assistance of the Board of Underwriters of New York in selecting the devices to be bought. Surfboats, corrugated iron life-cars, mortars, flares and various other odds and ends were acquired and Captain Ottinger erected small boathouses at selected points along the Jersey coast. Station #1 was located on Spermacetti Cove, near Sandy Hook. These early stations had no paid keepers or crew and were managed in a more or less slipshod manner.

The first appropriation affecting the Great Lakes was made in August of 1854 and provided $12,500 to purchase boats for twenty-five points along Lake Mighigan and other points to be determined by the Secretary of the Treasury. By the end of 1854 there were nine lifeboats on Lake Ontario, fourteen on Lake Erie, twenty-three on Lake Michigan, and only one on Lake Superior.

A complete lack of organization resulted in the neglect, disuse and abuse of the lifeboats, and the complete isolation of some stations made them easy prey for vandals and thieves. These deplorable conditions brought a storm of public protest when, in 1854, the *Powhatan* went down and 300 persons died.

This wave of indignation prompted Congress to appropriate new monies and provide for the appointment of a superintendent on the Long Island and New Jersey coasts and keepers for each station, to be paid $200 a year. No provision was made, however, for the employment of paid crews and the omission proved to be a serious flaw in the legislation for, although there were now paid keepers at each station, in the event of a wreck, a crew still had to be gathered. Often, the keeper had been appointed to his position as a political reward and the experienced surfmen refused to work for them. A second problem created by the use of volunteer crews was their lack of training and skill. Rescue work under adverse conditions required a great deal of teamwork and these "catch as catch can" crews were often highly inept.

Congress took little or no interest in the lifesaving services except to periodically allocate funds for their continuation. No regulations for the administration of the service were issued and there was no system of accountability for the money's use. Keepers were not even required to maintain records of shipwrecks or aid given. The mismanagement and disorganization continued for seventeen years.

The winter of 1870-71 was especially harsh and numerous fatal disasters were recorded. On the Great Lakes alone, 214 people perished. This tragic loss of life was attributed to a large extent to the ineptitude of the lifesaving crews and the inadequacy of their equipment. A new flurry of protests arose and a newly awakened Congress appropriated its largest single funding to date, $200,000 on April 20th, 1871 for the purpose of employing paid crews, building new stations and repairing equipment.

It is interesting to note that the early metamorphasis of the Service was due almost exclusively to disasters which so outraged the public as to result in positive legislation. For instance, a bill similar to the one passed April 20, 1871, calling for the employment of paid crews, had been defeated in 1869.

A Revenue Marine Bureau was reestablished by Secretary of the Treasury, George S. Boutwell, to administer both the cutters and the lifesaving stations. Sumner I. Kimball was appointed the civilian head of the Bureau on February 1, 1871.

Kimball determined that a complete restructuring of the Service was called for and detailed Captain John Faunce of the Revenue Cutter Service to make a thorough investigation of the condition of the stations, equipment and crews, to provide him with a better understanding of what measures would be needed.

An inveterate organizer, Kimball removed the incapable and inefficient officers from the Service, had stations repaired, equipment replaced and issued a series of regulations which established the responsibilities of crew-members and made everyone subject to discipline. He established qualifications for admission into the Service through examination, appointed inspectors to periodically check the stations for

Sumner I. Kimball, General Superintendent of the U. S. Life Saving Service, 1878-1915.

efficiency and instituted a systematic method for maintaining the stations. Reports and log books were required, a patrol system devised and an effective code of signals established.

March 24, 1873, Secretary Boutwell appointed Kimball, Faunce, and Captain J. H. Merryman to a commission to make a detailed report on the cost of erecting new stations and recommending sites. The commission interviewed underwriters, wreckers, shipowners, masters, custom officers and various others and personally inspected the coasts when deemed necessary.

The need for three classes of stations was reported to Congress January 29, 1874. First class stations (complete life saving stations) were estimated to cost $5,302 and would contain all the equipment necessary for rendering assistance to vessels at isolated points along the shore where there were few inhabitants. Full-time crews would man these stations.

Most of the stations along the Great Lakes were to be of the second class. These stations, erected at a cost of $4,790 would consist primarily of a lifeboat and a few other essential pieces of apparatus. Initially, it was proposed that these stations be manned by volunteer crews, paid for services rendered whenever they were needed. This classification of station was designed for densely populated areas where most marine disasters involved ships running aground or meeting some other misfortune in the vicinity of a harbor or pier where help was readily available.

A third class, the house of refuge, costing $2,995 was designed exclusively for use on the Florida coasts.

Congress referred the report to its Committee on Commerce which subsequently formulated the recommendations into a bill and on June 20, 1874 authorization was given to establish new stations of the various classes. The Act included: one complete lifesaving station and four lifeboat stations on Lake Erie; two complete and two lifeboat stations on Lake Ontario; four complete and one lifeboat station on Lake Huron; four complete stations on Lake Superior and, on Lake Michigan, three complete and nine lifeboat stations. A superintendent for each district was also authorized with one appointed for Lakes Erie and Ontario, one for Lakes Huron and Superior and one for Lake Michigan. They received $1,000 per year salary and performed the duties of customs inspectors. Station keepers were to be paid $200 yearly, crews at complete lifesaving stations were to receive not more than forty dollars per month and volunteer crews not more than ten dollars per rescue involving the saving of human life.

A further provision of the Act established two classes of medals of honor to be awarded for extreme and heroic endangerment of self by those rescuing or attempting to rescue persons in peril upon American waters or from American ships. The Director of the Mint was charged with selecting a design for the new medals. He invited the competition of artists to design the first class medal and was so impressed by that submitted by Anthony C. Paquet that he immediately commissioned him to furnish a design for the second class medal also.

A commission composed of the Chief of the Revenue Marine Bureau, the Chief of the Navigation Division and the Supervising Inspector-General of Steamboats was appointed to review claims for the award and forward their recommendations to the Secretary for final review.

A trio of brothers from Marblehead, Ohio

were the first to be awarded the first class medal on June 19, 1876. Lucien Clemons and his brothers Hubbard and A. J. received the award for their efforts in rescuing two crewmen from the *Consuelo* during a violent storm May 1, 1875. Later in 1876 when a station was established at Marblehead, Lucien Clemons was appointed keeper and remained in service until March 31, 1897.

It was in the centennial year of 1876 that the Life Saving Service actually began operating on the Great Lakes with the opening of the following stations:

Lakes Erie and Ontario
David P. Dobbins,
Superintendent

Station	Location	Date Opened
Oswego, NY Lake Ontario	Entrance to harbor	Sept. 28, 1876
Charlotte, NY Lake Ontario	Entrance to harbor	Oct. 2, 1876
Presque Isle, PA Lake Erie	Entrance to harbor	Oct. 6, 1876
Fairport, OH Lake Erie	Entrance to harbor	Oct. 10, 1876
Cleveland, OH Lake Erie	Entrance to harbor	Sept. 20, 1876
Point Marble-head	Near Quarry Docks	Sept. 20, 1876

Interior of the boathouse at the U. S. Life Saving Station, Oswego, shows at left a two-wheel breeches buoy rescue apparatus cart, and at right a life car on a four-wheel wagon chained to another two-wheel cart carrying lifeline apparatus. A horse and the crew supplied the power for pulling the carts and wagon. (Copied from an old photograph by Robert Oliphant of Oswego.)

Lakes Huron and Superior
Joseph Sawyer, Superintendent

Point Aux Barques, MI Lake Huron	Near lighthouse	Sept. 15, 1876
Ottawa Point (Tawas) Lake Huron	Near lighthouse	Oct. 6, 1876
Sturgeon Point, MI Lake Huron	Near lighthouse	Sept. 15, 1876
Thunder Bay Island Lake Huron	Near lighthouse	Sept. 25, 1876
Forty Mile Point (Hammond's Bay) Lake Huron	Near lighthouse	Sept. 30, 1876

Vermilion, Michigan Station was the most isolated station in the Eleventh District. One of the original Great Lakes stations it was erected and placed in commission in 1876.

There also were stations established in 1876 which did not begin actual operations until the opening of navigation the following year. These included:

Lakes Ontario and Erie

Big Sandy Creek, NY Lake Ontario	North side of creek mouth	April 16, 1877
Salmon Creek, NY Lake Ontario	East side of creek mouth	April 1, 1877
Buffalo, NY Lake Erie	Entrance to harbor	April, 1877

Lakes Huron and Superior

Vermillion Pt., MI Lake Superior	10 miles west of White Fish Point	May 15, 1877
Crisps, MI Lake Superior	18 miles west of White Fish Point	May 15, 1877
Two Heart River, MI Lake Superior	Near mouth of river	May 15, 1877
Sucker River, MI Lake Superior	Near mouth of river	May 15, 1877

Lake Michigan
Eugene W. Watson, Superintendent

North Manitou Island Lake Michigan	Near Packard's Wharf	June 23, 1877
Point au Bec Scies Lake Mighigan	Near lighthouse	April 23, 1877
Grand Point au Sable Lake Michigan	Near lighthouse	May 15, 1877
Grand Haven, MI Lake Michigan	Entrance to harbor	May 1, 1877
St. Joseph, MI Lake Michigan	In harbor	May 1, 1877
Old Chicago, IL Lake Michigan	In harbor	May 25, 1877
Racine, WI Lake Michigan	In harbor	June 2, 1877
Milwaukee, WI Lake Michigan	Near harbor entrance	May 7, 1877
Sheboygan, WI Lake Michigan	Entrance to harbor	May 4, 1877
Two Rivers, WI Lake Michigan	Entrance to harbor	May 1, 1877

The Great Lakes became the Ninth, Tenth, and Eleventh Districts with headquarters at Buffalo, Detroit, and Grand Haven. Superintendents were responsible for selecting the keepers, who, in turn were to select the crews. Both keepers and crews were examined by a board of inspectors comprised of an officer of the Revenue Cutter Service, a surgeon of the Marine Hospital Service and an expert surfman to determine their health, character and skill. Keepers were required to be able-bodied, of good character and habits, able to read and write and under forty-five years of age with a thorough mastery of boat craft and surfing.

Once appointed, the keeper was required to permanently reside at the station. He was responsible for the care and custody of the station property and grounds, had absolute authority over his crew, was an ex-officio customs inspector and was responsible for all shipwrecked property until it was retrieved by the owner or the agent. On rescues where boats were used, he manned the steering oar and directed the operations.

The number of men composing the crew was determined by the number of oars needed to pull the largest boat used at the station. Normally this was six but many of the Lakes' stations used the self-righting and self-bailing lifeboat which required an eight-man crew. Crews were selected by the keepers from the experienced, able-bodied surfmen who lived in the vicinity of the station. Regulations would later prohibit a keeper from employing nepotism in the selection of his crew. Upon entering the service, a surfman could be no older than forty-five and had to be physically fit and highly skilled. He was required to live at the station during the entire "active season", which for the Great Lakes, normally meant from April 15 to December 15.

Surfmen were ranked by order of experience and skill with the most competent man being Number 1 and the least experienced Number 6 or 8. Each man had a specific duty, with which he was required to be thoroughly familiar, for every type of drill the Service performed. Detailed accounts of some of these drills will be given later.

By June 18, 1878, the merits of this totally reorganized Service were recognized by Congress and on that date, the Life Saving Service was made a separate entity under the Department of the Treasury. President Rutherford B. Hayes appointed Sumner Kimball as General Superintendent. There was no restriction imposed on the number of years which a General Superintendent could serve and Mr. Kimball became the only man ever to hold that position, remaining in office until 1915 when his Service merged with the Revenue Cutter Service to form the U. S. Coast Guard.

There is a tendency in many histories to record the facts and overlook the personalities and yet, had it not been for the personalities, the facts might well have been different. During the days when the Life Saving Service was emerging from its infancy, a number of men, whose contributions had heretofore been of little significance, were suddenly thrust into the spotlight and recognized as shapers of history.

One such individual was George Francis Babcock, the first Keeper of the Fairport Life Saving Station. Born in Fairport, December 20, 1845, Babcock began his sailing career in 1863 and served aboard several vessels before being appointed Assistant Keeper of the lighthouse in 1871. When the Life Saving Service came to Fairport in 1876, David P. Dobbins, Superintendent of the newly-formed Ninth District, named Babcock as Keeper of the station based on his experience as commander of the volunteer crew already in operation. Keeper Babcock continued working with the volunteer crew until legislation provided a permanent, paid crew. In his twenty-two years as Keeper, his station was responsible for rescuing more than 300 people.

Other heroes of the Service were Frederick T. Hatch, one of the few men in history to receive the Gold Life saving Medal twice, Jerome Kiah, holder of the Gold Medal, later Superintendent of the Tenth Life Saving District, Keeper Charles C. Goodwin and his entire crew of the Cleveland Life Saving Station, every one of whom received the Gold Lifesaving Medal, Ingar Olsen of the Milwaukee Station, also awarded the Gold Medal and a long list of keepers and surfmen who, although not honored for their heroism, were well-renowned along the Lake coasts for their didicated service and bravery.

Within a very short space of time, the Life Saving Service had become legendary. Many of the contemporary journalists referred to its members as "Heroes of the Surf", "Storm Warriors" and similar glowing terms. The surfmen were pictured as "Arthurian Knights", calmly sitting around their stations awaiting news of a disaster where their special skills would be daringly exhibited and ultimately save the day. Indeed, the dramatic and thrilling accounts of a surfman's life were inspiring but only partially true. Although the lifesavers did perform feats of unparalleled heroism when the need arose, their daily lives can best be described as tedious.

The normal life of a surfman during the active season usually centered around drilling and becoming skilled in the use of his equipment and the regular upkeep required to keep the station and its equipment in good operating order.

Each day except Sunday, the surfmen could be found drilling or cleaning. Some drills, especially the beach apparatus drill with its firing of the Lyle gun, drew large crowds of spectators. The beach apparatus was regarded as one of the most important pieces of equipment the Service used. It was designed to rescue those shipwrecked within 600 yards of the shore when rough seas precluded the launching of a boat. The main components of this apparatus were a small, bronze, cannon-like gun (the Lyle gun), projectiles, small messenger line, large hawser ropes, a breeches buoy and other miscellaneous bits of equipment. The apparatus was mounted aboard a wagon or cart known as the "beach cart", which was pulled by the surfmen themselves or by horses.

With the command "Action", the cart was started toward the drill location, usually an area of beach adjacent to the station. Once on scene, the keeper would set up the cannon while ropes and other equipment were laid out. He'd then select the proper amount of powder, size line and projectile. The messenger line, stored in a pegged wooden box, called a faking box, required a good deal of skill to properly coil the line around the pegs without snarling it. When everything was ready, the keeper would tie the messenger line to the projectile, adjust the elevation of the gun, attach the firing lanyard, stand back and pull. With a large roar and an even larger cloud of smoke, the projectile would fly toward the target, the messenger line feeding rapidly out of the faking box. During these drills, the keeper's target was a pole shaped like a ship's mast. After the messenger line was affixed to the mast, a hawser was drawn out and a breeches buoy rigged.

So important did the Service consider this drill, that it required crews to practice it twice each week on Monday and Thursday. A crew was expected to perform the entire drill in five minutes or less and this need for speed caused a spirited rivalry to arise among the stations, each station striving to be best in the District. According to Superintendent Kimball, amazing times of two minutes were achieved. This rivalry then, served not only to raise esprit de corps but it also developed the proficient teamwork so necessary in rescue work on a dark, stormy night when speed and efficiency were often the difference between life and death.

Tuesday's drill was usually the most impressive to spectators and was so popular that crews often performed it for special community affairs and celebrations. The drill itself consisted of launching the surfboat and then after practicing pulling oars in the surf for about thirty minutes, the crew would deliberately capsize their boat, right it and continue rowing. This deliberate tipping over of the boat was designed to condition the men to react properly when an angry surf picked up a boat and literally hurled it upside down. A perennial crowd-pleaser, one observer described the scene this way: "No sight is more impressive".

There were primarily two types of boats used by the Life Saving Service: a self-bailing, self-righting, 700-1,000 pound boat pulled by six surfmen and the two or four ton lifeboat. This latter boat was also self-bailing and self-righting but was designed for use in heavy weather and could be fitted with sails. Its great weight limited its use to the Great Lakes and Pacific Coast where there were launchways into deep water.

Two other drills occupied the remainder of the week, signal drill and "restoring the apparently drowned". Signal drill consisted of each surfman being examined on his knowledge of the meanings of the various flags, the definitions of two, three and four flag hoists, the distinguishing flag or pennant of each hoist, use of the code book and actual practice in using the codes. The men of the Life Saving Service became so skilled in the use of these signals that many of them were transferred to the Army Signal Corps during the Spanish-American War.

The "restoration of the apparently drowned" involved practicing the method of resuscitation known as the "direct method" devised by Dr. Marshall Hall and Dr. H. R. Silvester, and becoming acquainted with the use of the medicine chest in administering first aid.

Beach apparatus drill showing all equipment set up. Crewmembers may be seen ready to get into breeches buoy.

Beach apparatus drill remained an integral part of the Service as shown in this 1940 photo.

David A. Lyle—inventor of the Line Throwing Gun, (U. S. Army photo.)

Saturdays were devoted to cleaning the station and any "free time" the men had between drills, assistance calls and patrolling, was used for keeping the equipment up and doing the other odd jobs necessary for smooth operation of the station.

The Lyle Gun was still in use in 1957.

Life Saving crew pulling beach cart at North Manitou Station, 1893.

Day watch at the stations were kept from sunrise to sunset by a surfman who was assigned to the lookout tower. There were no seats in the tower which kept the watch-standers more alert and they were obliged to ring a bell each half hour to let the keeper know they were attending to business. A log was also kept by the lookout in which he would note the number of vessels seen passing, weather conditions, wind direction and temperature.

39

At night, the watch took the form of beach patrols with the first watch being from sunset to 8 p.m. and followed by three other watches from 8-12, 12-4, and 4 to sunrise. Beach patrol was performed by two surfmen who, at the beginning of their designated watch, set out from the station in opposite directions, keeping as near as possible to the shoreline. Patrol distances ranged up to five miles one way, and the beaches were often "clad with ice" and were at best "pathless deserts in the night." Each surfman carried a lantern and Coston Signals, the flare-like signalling device used by the Service to warn vessels approaching too close to the beach or to let shipwrecked sailors know they had been spotted and help was on the way.

Plodding "through the soft sand, in spite of flooding tides, bewildering snowfalls, overwhelming winds, and bitter cold," the surfman reached a halfway house. There he exchanged a check with the patrolman from the next station to prove to the keeper on his return that he had "faithfully performed his allotted task." If, after arriving at the halfway house, the other patrolman didn't show up, the patrolman started toward the other station to see if some mishap had befallen his comrade. At stations too far apart to have the patrolmen meet, the surfman would carry a special clock. Upon reaching the limits of his patrol, he would find a key attached to a post. This key would make an impression on the dial of the clock, showing the exact time when a surfman was at his post.

Giving the signal—Coston flares were used to warn off ships too close to shore.

Many a dramatic rescue began with the patrolman excitedly running to alert the keeper of a vessel in distress and the importance of the patrol was also graphically illustrated during the active season of 1899 when the surfmen's Coston Signals were credited with warning off 143 vessels in danger of running aground. Surfmen on patrol duty were not excused from their other obligations. Regardless of how exhausting a patrol had been, if a wreck occurred, the patrolman was obliged to take up his regular post with the crew.

Although the exploits of these lifesavers were often over-romanticized, they most certainly were hardy men of great dedication. They endured innumerable hardships during the "active season", for which they received a paltry $65.00 per month (originally it was $40) and when the season was over they were made to shift for themselves. On the Great Lakes, the active season lasted about eight months, which meant that the surfmen had to seek other jobs for the remaining four months. The term of enlistment for surfmen was for a single season. Each spring, they had to be re-examined and the slightest defect could end a twenty-year career, without pension. Should a surfman have been unfortunate enough to perish in the line of duty, his family received no compensation or if he were disabled, he received nothing at all. Still, the Service was able to attract men who were "hardy and able seamen, dexterous and courageous, matchless in managing boats in heavy seas and in the perilous neighborhood of wrecks, and of such approved integrity that the property of mariners and passengers, and the cargoes of vessels saved by their efforts, suffer no loss at their hands".

Most stations were originally two-story buildings with a small, lookout tower on the roof peak. The first floor consisted of four rooms, a boat room where the apparatus was kept, a mess-room, a storeroom and the keeper's room. Two rooms occupied the second story; one was used as quarters for the crew while the other contained spare cots for sheltering rescued persons and doubled as a storage space.

Those Lake stations located at the harbors had an inclined platform which extended from the boat room to the water. Two tramways were laid on the platform to facilitate launching the heavier boats which were kept mounted on cradles or cars. In the rear of the building there was an exit for the surfboat wagon and beach apparatus cart should they need to be transported along the shore. After 1880, horses were also provided at stations to transport these heavy carts.

Artist's conception of a typical Life Saving Station in the late 19th Century.

Unlike other Services, the Life Saving Service was primarily a local affair. Surfmen had to be residents of the District in which they enlisted and could live no more than five miles inland. Once the Service became established, keepers were selected from among the surfmen at the station where a vacancy existed. Usually the Number 1 Surfman became keeper. Superintendents were promoted from the most experienced keepers in the District. Thus, the Life Saving Service not only served the communities in which they were located, they were part of those communities. In some towns along the coast, the citizenry were so proud of their lifesaving stations and their crews that, each year at Christmas, the neighbors closest to the stations would throw a gala dinner to honor them, complete with musicians, dancing and "a feast fit for a king".

As we have pointed out in earlier accounts of the Lighthouse Service, whole families were sometimes called upon to render assistance to those in distress. The Life Saving Service was no different. One example of this family dedication involves S. W. Morgan, Keeper of the Grand Point au Sable Life Saving Station. Keeper Morgan's son James, interrupted his own successful maritime career to become the Number 1 Surfman on his father's crew, serving four years before being appointed Keeper of the Manistee Station. The pair was involved in many a heroic rescue, but it was Edith Morgan, the elder Keeper's daughter and James' younger sister, whose heroism on two occasions earned the Silver Life Saving Medal. The story of the Morgans is by no means a singular occurrence, for the records of the Service are replete with similar accounts.

By 1893 there were forty-seven stations along the Great Lakes. The Service was expanding rapidly but so was dissatisfaction with the administration. The country was sinking into a serious economic depression. Farm prices had plunged steadily downward, factories had closed, thousands were unemployed and the shrinking gold reserves threatened to create runaway inflation.

Surfmen were receiving only $50 per month and this only during the active season. They were still obliged to seek other jobs during the remaining four months. To this was added the growing public dissatisfaction with the spoils system, which cast all public servants in the role of political hacks and caused suspicions to arise as to the qualifications of the surfmen.

With widespread suspicion resulting in an almost continuous barrage of accusations of incompetence being levied against the lifesavers, fewer sailors and surfmen were willing to enlist in the Service while the shrinking job market and tight money was causing the experienced but underpaid keepers and surfmen to seek better paying jobs. The Great Lakes was especially affected by this rising tide of discontentment and in 1893, more than thirty percent of the total amount of keepers and surfmen in the three Lakes districts, resigned.

This period of unrest and dissatisfaction continued until an Executive Order issued May 6, 1896 brought the Life Saving Service under the rules of the Civil Service. Although the first admission of an applicant to the Service under these rules was not made until April 1, 1897, many initial difficulties were encountered during the transition period.

Some of these early problems can be laid at the feet of the new breed of "yellow journalists". Sensationalism in newspaper reporting had just become vogue during this period and along the Great Lakes, the press so badly misrepresented the effect of Civil Service on the Life Saving Service that a great deal of friction was spawned and delayed the full implementation of the new rules.

One of the most serious incidents involved a newspaper story which reported that the Great Lakes Districts were in a deplorable condition since the advent of Civil Service. The story claimed that those men capable of passing the mental tests were not physically fit and those

41

who had served for years prior to the implementation of Civil Service, could not pass the mental tests and had been dismissed. It said the Service had become so disorganized that lighthouse tender crews had to be used in their place whenever there was a rescue to be made.

Although the Treasury Department knew the reports to be false, they asked the three District Superintendents to submit a "frank statement" giving their own opinion of the effect of the new rules on the efficiency and welfare of the Service. All three resoundingly decried the press reports to be false with the Ninth District Superintendent adding ". . . the discipline, efficiency, and personnel of the station crews are far superior to what they were a few years since, and I have yet to hear the first word of criticism against them from the local public".

As time progressed and the rules became better understood, the furor died down and more applications were received until once more there was an adequate number of men assigned and an equally adequate number available. By December 1, 1898, a period of twenty months after the first applicant had been accepted, 389 surfmen were appointed, only seventeen of whom were subsequently discharged as being unsatisfactory.

The technological revolution came to the Life Saving Service via the Great Lakes in 1899, when Keeper Henry Cleary and his crew began the shift from manpower to mechanical power at the Marquette (Michigan) Station. Steam had never been a viable solution to the problem of lifeboat propulsion, since steam engines required a power plant that was both too bulky and too heavy for the small boats and could be easily extinguished in rough weather. The development of the internal combustion engine in the latter part of the nineteenth century, however, gave the promise of being an answer to the surfman's needs.

Lieutenant C. H. McLellan, "a revenue cutter officer and experienced researcher in life saving materiel," combined with Keeper Cleary's crew and the Lake Shore Engine Works to launch the first motor lifeboat. The prototype was a 34-foot lifeboat equipped with a two cylinder, twelve horsepower Superior engine. Trials of the motor lifeboat were conducted during September 1899 and were successful enough to encourage the Secretary of the Treasury to appoint a commission to study the general topic of mechanized lifeboats and their

design and to formulate a recommendation. Headed by Professor C. H. Peabody of the Massachusetts Institute of Technology, the commission strongly recommended the use of power boats. A full-scale mechanization program was implemented in 1905 and by year's end, twelve boats were in operation.

36' Motor Lifeboat—mainstay of early 20th Century search and rescue efforts.

The motorized lifeboats greatly extended the range of operations of the stations and their speed in responding to calls for assistance. Telephones, telegraphs and eventually radios were added to the technological revamping of the Service. As a result of this modernization program, many stations were no longer required and were abandoned and still others were relocated to more advantageous sites.

In 1900, sixty stations were operating along the Great Lakes. In the Ninth District, stations had been added at Fort Niagara, New York; Ashtabula, Ohio; Lake View Beach, Harbor

Beach, Port Austin, and Middle Island, Michigan. New facilities in the Tenth District included: Bois Blanc, Charlevoix, South Manitou Island, Sleeping Bear Point, Frankfort, Manistee, Ludington, Pentwater, White River, Muskegon, Holland, and South Haven, Michigan and Michigan City, Indiana. Eleventh District additions were at South Chicago and Jackson Park, Illinois; Kenosha, Kewaunee, Sturgeon Bay Canal, Bailey Harbor, and Plum Island, Wisconsin; Grand Marais, Pere Marquette, and Portage, Michigan; and Duluth, Minnesota.

Uniforms were not required in the Service until August 5, 1889. At that time a circular was issued which prescribed the uniform for surfmen and keepers and required its purchase. These regulations were amended April 5, 1895. A keeper's uniform consisted of a dark indigo-blue, double-breasted coat of either kersey or flannel with matching vest and trousers. A dark blue cloth cap with visor and chin strap was also required. The Service's symbol, a life buoy, crossed and interlocked oar and boathook embroidered in gold was worn on the center of the band with the letters "U. S." above and "L.S.S." below. Keepers wore gilt buttons with the symbol embossed.

Surfmen's uniforms were similar to those of keepers but were single-breasted and did not include a vest. On the right coat sleeve they wore an emblem embroidered in white silk upon a dark blue square. The surfmen's number was also on a dark blue square and was worn on the left sleeve midway between the shoulder and the elbow. Caps for surfmen had no chinstrap, but instead a 1½ inch wide black silk ribbon with "U. S. LIFE SAVING SERVICE" printed in one inch gold block letters. Plain black buttons were worn by the surfmen.

Members of the Life Saving Service were obliged to pay for their own uniforms. A complete uniform for keepers could be purchased for about $20 with an overcoat also available for $17. A surfman's uniform was about $5 less.

Assistant District Inspectors were responsible for ordering the uniforms and forwarding payment to the manufacturers.

We will not detail the hundreds of thrilling rescues performed by the Life Saving Service, for that would fill several volumes. However, after declaring the lifesavers the real makers of history, we would be remiss if we failed to cite a few of the more extraordinary incidents.

On the 24th of November 1882, a sudden northwest gale wreaked havoc all across the Great Lakes, leaving a trail of death and destruction in its wake. The schooner *J. O. Moss*, bound for her homeport of Chicago with a six-man crew and a cargo of shingles, was anchored about four miles north of the Grand Point au Sable Station (Lake Michigan) when the storm struck. She was easy prey for the killer storm, having been struck hard the previous day by another gale. A patrolman from the station spotted her about 3:00 a.m. and hurried back to alert the keeper. At daybreak, just as the Life Saving crew arrived at the scene, the *Moss*, caught in the raging gale and swirling snow, parted her chain and spun around, rolling wildly until finally she grounded about 500 yards from shore.

Leaving Surfman Stillson on the beach, the crew hastened back to the station for their beach apparatus. Hauling the gear by hand was impractical, so it was necessary to secure a team of horses from Ludington before the crew could return and rescue the six men trapped in the *Moss'* rigging.

Stillson, meanwhile, kept a lonely vigil on the distressed ship, which continued to roll wildly in the pounding surf. The men had climbed out of the rigging by now and a horrified Stillson could see that one of them had attached a line to himself and was attempting to reach shore in a yawl. Frantically, the surfman tried vainly to dissuade him, yelling that help was on the way. The boat was soon swamped in foam and capsized, leaving the sailor to struggle helplessly for his life. Fearing the man would drown, Stillson valiantly plunged into the swirling waters and pulled him ashore. Although unconscious, the man soon revived next to the fire the alert surfman had built. He then secured the boat, which had drifted ashore to a heavy log while the sailors on board the schooner fastened their end, making the line taut. Not long after, the vessel's mate Barney McDonald, thinking he could aid the rescuers, began making his way, hand over hand on the suspended line, to shore. The hours of exposure to the freezing cold and gale took their toll and after managing only twenty-five yards, the exhausted mate slipped from the line and was swallowed up by the angry sea.

At eleven o'clock, the Life Saving crew arrived with their apparatus. It had taken them more than an hour to reach the scene after getting the team from Ludington because the beach was so strewn with debris that they had been forced to travel along the sandhills. Soft, yielding sand precluded a rapid transit, yet with a remarkable effort the crew struggled to reach the wreck. Once they arrived, it didn't take long to rescue the remaining four men, but the rolling of the vessel prevented the hauling taut of the hawser lines and each of the rescued, riding ashore in the breeches buoy, was in and out of the freezing water. They proved to be so exhausted, drenched and insensible that at first the lifesavers thought they were dead. A warm fire, blankets and some brandy soon restored their vitality and no one was seriously injured.

Going through the breakers to rescue crew of a stranded vessel.

Captain Davis, the *Moss'* skipper, had nothing but praise for Keeper Shanty Morgan and his crew, adding "God bless the life-saving service! is the prayer of my men and myself." Edward Cody, the vessel's owner, also spoke highly of the crew and the Eleventh District Inspector who investigated the disaster proclaimed that their actions ". . . only served to reflect credit and glory on the conduct of Captain (sic) Shanty Morgan and his crew of life-savers" and the loss of McDonald ". . . was no fault of Captain Morgan's men". These thoughts were echoed by the press which concluded their accounts of the disaster, ". . . it is known that the life-saving crews were faithful and fearless in the discharge of their dangerous duty."

Artist's view of a Life Saving Service crew rescuing a shipwrecked sailor.

While McDonald had been making his way along the line, a somewhat similar incident was occurring only five miles away. The same gale which had driven the *Moss* to anchor the previous day had also brought disaster to the *Eclipse*. Bound for Chicago like the *Moss*, *Eclipse* was also a schooner, laden with shingles and manned by a crew of six. Her cargo had shifted and partially capsized the vessel before she finally grounded about four hundred feet from shore. The crew had been forced to take to the rigging, where they spent the night, pelted by a driving snow and flying seas until they were nearly frozen. Completely exhausted by morning, the crew held little hope of rescue, and so it was decided to send one man ashore for help. Anton Rasmusson was the poor unfortunate whose efforts proved as futile as McDonald's had been.

About noon, two hunters caught sight of the *Eclipse* and hastily went off in search of the lifesavers. It was an hour and a half later when the tired hunters came across the station crew returning from the wrecked *J. O. Moss*. Immediately, the men turned about and began the nine mile trek to where the *Eclipse* had run aground. This second trip with the gear proved much harsher than the first, as they had to again proceed up and down the soft, yielding sand of the dunes, while plunging through thick underbrush and fallen trees. It was an arduous journey and to add to the misery, one of the horses gave out and also had to be helped along. Finally, just before dark (about 7:00 p.m.) they arrived, and aided by the blazing fire started by the two hunters who had preceded them, they set about firing a line to the *Eclipse*. Within an hour, the five survivors had been brought safely ashore and it was learned the twenty-five year old Rasmusson was to have been married in Chicago on Thanksgiving, making his death even more tragic, for had he not tried to make it to shore, he most surely would have been saved.

The gallant efforts of the Grand Point au Sable crew on November 24th were cited in the Service's *Annual Report* for Fiscal Year 1883:

> The labors of the life-saving crew upon this date seem particularly worthy of honorable comment. They performed the remarkable service of saving life from two wrecks in succession with the same apparatus; working . . . with wet and frozen lines, which it required peculiar skill and judgement to handle effectively. To achieve this end involved a severe trudge . . . , of thirty-four miles, trundling with the aid of half-blown horses, a heavy wagon . . . , through a rough wilderness of brush and sand and with the concomitants of a battering gale and blasts of snow. The . . . setting up hawsers and hauling lines, and dragging upon them in the drench of icy surf . . . , becomes a mere incident to the savage toils of such a journey.

One of the most extraordinary series of near catastrophes and narrow escapes took place in November, 1883 when a ferocious gale, "the curse of the eleventh month", caused widespread destruction along the coasts of the Lakes from Chicago to Lake Ontario. The story, however, began almost a week earlier on November 7th with the schooner *Arab* grounding near St. Joseph, Michigan. Both crew and cargo were saved by the crew of the Life Saving Station there and as soon as the seas had calmed, a steam pump was brought aboard to attempt refloating the vessel. Another pump was needed, which arrived aboard the tug *Protection*. After the leaks had been temporarily patched, the *Protection* set out for Milwaukee with the *Arab* in tow.

There were eighteen men aboard the two vessels when they left St. Joseph about 7:00 p.m., confident the two steam pumps would be capable of handling the calm seas. The seas, however, did not remain calm. About thirty miles from Racine, the two vessels were struck with the full fury of the November gale. No longer could the beleagured pumps keep back the flow of water and the *Arab* suddenly lurched, rolled over and went down. William Kelly, the pump engineer, was crushed by a falling pump. A small boat from the *Protection* saved the remaining crew, but as the tug backed down to retrieve the rescued, she caught the towing line in her wheel and became disabled.

Fifteen men aboard the *Protection* were now at the mercy of the ever increasing gale. About 9:30 that morning, five hours after the *Arab* had gone under, the steambarge *H. C. Akeley* appeared on the horizon and responded to the tug's plea for help. By 11:00 she was in tow, but the wind had now undergone a sudden change in direction and the two vessels labored in the swirling sea until 4:00 p.m. when the *Akeley's* rudder gave way. Valiantly they tried to hold on, but by 7:00 in the evening, the *Akeley's* cargo had shifted and she rolled partially over on her side. The tow line was cast off and both vessels drifted off. The *Akeley* later lost her smoke stack, and main and mizzen sail and at 1:30 the next afternoon, foundered stern first. Six crewmen were lost, including the Captain and First Mate. The rest were saved after an extraordinary effort by the crew of the disabled schooner *Driver*.

All this time, the tug *Protection* had been drifting perilously in the angry seas until she beached off Saugatuck. A call for help went out to the Life Saving Station at Grand Haven, but their crew was out on another rescue, leaving the St. Joseph Station as the only hope for the battered tug. Keeper Stevens promptly loaded his crew, boat and beach apparatus aboard a train bound for Richmond, forty miles to the north, where they were met by the tug *Ganges* and carried the remaining thirteen miles to Saugatuck. The lifesavers arrived around 5:00 p.m., but were unable to get a line out to the tug—it was too far out. Blowing snow, fierce winds and heavy seas kept them from launching a boat. All they could do was watch helplessly and wait. Again the wind changed and pushed the battered *Protection* into the breakers. Four hours after arriving on scene, Keeper Stevens was able to land a line on the tug. Quickly, a breeches buoy was rigged and one by one, the survivors of the two ships were hauled ashore. All were saved except Kelly, who went down with the *Arab*, and a young fireman who had become impatient and tried to swim ashore. The heroic efforts of the St. Joseph Life Saving crew, who had travelled fifty-three miles to rescue the men on the *Protection* and who had stood in icy water for over an hour until all were ashore, were the subject of many glowing stories for weeks after.

Long after paid crews were employed by the Life Saving Service, civilian volunteers remained an important element in rescues; often

45

seconding the efforts of the regular crew by their gallant actions. One incident of this spirit involved a double rescue off the coast of Cleveland, Ohio, in the merging days of October and November, 1883.

A three-master schooner, the *Sophia Minch*, trying to outrun a northwesterly gale, began her run into Cleveland Harbor about 7:00 on the evening of October 31st. Her attempt failed, as the pounding seas snapped her rudder and forced her to drop anchor and signal for assistance. The tug *Peter Smith* soon came alongside, with two members of the Life Saving crew aboard, but had to return to the harbor because the *Minch's* Captain was doubtful that one tug could handle the load and refused to heave anchor. Keeper Goodwin of the Cleveland Station took his crew aboard the *Smith* and accompanied by the *Fanny Tuthill*, they headed back to the *Minch*. It took some treacherous maneuvering in the raging swells, but the crew finally managed to board the disabled *Minch* and set up the tow lines. Not long after the two tugs had started pulling toward the breakwater, the heavy, pounding Lake proved too much. Both lines parted and the tugs scurried to safety.

Minch's hold began filling as the mountainous seas washed over her and she started dragging toward shore. A decision was made to scuttle her and take to the fore rigging. Two men were forced to seek refuge in the mizzen rigging as the crashing waves cut off their flight to the foremast.

Surfman Distel, who had been aboard the tug when the lines parted, was now safely ashore, but immediately set about to gather some volunteers to aid him in rescuing his fellows. His search found only five men who were willing to turn to in a raging storm at two o'clock in the morning. Customs Inspector Bates, George Tower, the lighthouse keeper, and three civilians: Pryor, Duffy and Tovat, proved to be enough, though. Aided by a team supplied by Tovat, within minutes they had carried the gear to a point opposite the *Minch*. Shortly, the men in the fore rigging had all been brought ashore but one lifesaver, Surfman Hatch, remained on board to assist the rescue of the two men now huddled nervously in the mizzen rigging.

Distel and Hatch agreed that should Hatch fail to return within a reasonable time, Distel was to head for shore. It was a perilous journey for Hatch, as he had to dodge both the heavy seas sweeping the deck below him and the swinging main boom and gaff sweeping the air above him. Somehow, he made his way aft and found both men safe, but he knew the three could never make it back to the line. All they could do was wait—and pray.

Distel had returned to shore as agreed and quickly the gear was reset, a shot fired to the aft section, and the three men swung to safety on the breeches buoy.

The heroism of Surfman Hatch is undisputed and legendary. He was twice awarded the Gold Lifesaving Medal. Keeper Goodwin and the rest of his crew would all receive the Gold Lifesaving Medal for their services during the 1883-1884 season and as for the civilians, the names Duffy, Tovat and Pryor would be seen often in newspaper accounts of rescues in Cleveland Harbor which gave "unmeasured praise" to both the lifesavers and their hardy band of volunteers.

One of the most disastrous storms on Lake Michigan began on May 21, 1883. Winds had been favorable for three or four days and a large fleet was downbound from Chicago to Milwaukee. Suddenly, a severe and unseasonable gale caught the masters by surprise and although in severity, the storm was not unprecedented nor unusual, the complete lack of warning resulted in extraordinary damage, especially to small craft and vessels not equipped to cope with rough weather. Several wrecks were driven ashore attempting to make the harbor. Happily, the loss of life was light, due mainly to the actions of the Life Saving crew and the splendid cooperation given them by the citizenry. The *Evening Wisconsin* of Milwaukee described the rescue efforts as "a needed and noble service by brave men."

One of the most notable rescues that day began about 8:30 in the evening as the schooner *Lillie E.* arrived in the tremendous seas off Milwaukee. No tug being in the bay, Captain James Brooks, her skipper, decided to sail his vessel into the harbor. Unfortunately, he could not hold his vessel in the rampaging waves and missed the harbor, violently sheering into the end of the south pier. Luckily, she had struck with the bluff of her port bow and sustained little damage, except the loss of her bobstays and cathead. The savage seas carried her past the south pier and she beached about a mile south of the Life Saving Station. Promptly, Keeper John Evensen and his crew made their way to the scene in their lifeboat, dragging the boat across Jone's Island in order to get a better position for launching a line. After tremendous difficulty, the seven-man crew of the *Lillie E.* was brought ashore; many had frozen hands and feet because of the weather's severity.

Throughout the day and into the night, the crews and volunteers worked feverishly to save stranded vessels and their men. So severe was the violence of the wind that lumber from the deck-load of the *Sailor Boy*, a grounded schooner, was blown clear across Jone's Island. In all, twenty-six ships had sought the refuge of Milwaukee Harbor, many of them damaged. It was said the Life Saving crew more than earned a year's salary in that one day. Only three lives were lost, and those were due to a mutiny aboard the schooner *Petrel*. The crew deserted the Captain and his ship and three men drowned as their yawl was capsized in the furious sea.

The "curse of the eleventh month" continued to plague the Great Lakes into the Twentieth Century. One of the most notable rescues took place during what has come to be known as the "Great Storm of 1913". During the height of that unforgettable tempest, twenty ships and two hundred and forty-eight persons were lost, many without a trace.

A steam-powered, steel-hulled ore carrier, the *L. C. Waldo* was among the vessels trapped by eighty mile an hour winds and driving snow. Mercilessly, the smashing seas and tremendous winds carried away the pilothouse and deckhouse, washing away the ship's navigational equipment and extinguishing her powerplants. With neither guidance nor power, the *Waldo's* fate was left to the storm. The giant waves, as if somehow angered by this 451-foot toy, lifted its almost 4,500 tons and hurled it solidly onto Gull Rock, off Manitou Island in Keweenaw Point (Lake Superior). Before long, she broke in two and the twenty-four men and two women were forced to retreat to the shelter of the windlass room, the vessel's highest point.

Manitou Island, at this time of year, was deserted and the *Waldo* carried no wireless. Death seemed imminent until the *George Stephenson*, a passing steamer spotted the wreck. Unable to render aid himself, Captain Mosher continued on until he reached the safety of Bete Grise Bay where he put ashore a boat and contacted the Life Saving Station at Eagle Harbor.

Unfortunately, the motor lifeboat at Eagle Harbor was being repaired and only an eight h.p. surfboat was available. Nonetheless, Keeper Tucker set out into the gale, only to be driven back by the storm and an iced-up boat. With no other recourse, the crew began an around-the-clock effort to repair their motor lifeboat and two days later, were finally able to get underway.

While the Eagle Harbor boat was being repaired, a second station, at Portage Ship Canal, also had received the call for help and had launched their boat and begun the 75-mile trek to Gull Rock. It was rough going for the Portage boat and in the first hour, they managed to travel only about one mile from the station. An alternate route was chosen through the somewhat sheltered waters of a ship canal. It was longer, but there was more chance for success this way. Collin Westrope described the journey in his report:

... the waves smashed against the bow and shook us like a dog shaking water off his back. ... In the troughs, the boat stood on her nose with the propeller out of the water, racing in the air.

At dawn on November 11th, four days after the *Waldo* had run aground, the Portage boat arrived, followed a short while later by the Eagle Harbor boat. Stiff from the cold, hungry and nearly exhausted, the two crews set about the job of rescuing the survivors, who were all huddled together in the windlass room. The lifesavers had to chop their way through a wall of ice, which solidly covered the hatchway before finding the crew, ". . . so haggard and worn from starvation and lack of sleep that they were more dead than alive, and their faces were ghostly white from frostbite." It took more than two hours of work to evacuate all the survivors, with everyone in almost constant peril from the treacherous seas and winds. Finally, it was over. The *Waldo* survivors were taken by tug to Houghton, Michigan, where they were rushed to a hospital. Everyone had been saved, thanks to the dedication and heroism of these two crews of lifesavers. On July 15, 1914, in recognition of the hardships and dangers undergone by the seven men from Eagle Harbor and the eight-man crew from Portage Ship Canal, they were all awarded the Gold Lifesaving Medal by the Secretary of the Treasury. Receiving the award were Charles A.

Tucker, Anthony F. Glaza, Thomas W. Bennetts, Serge Anderson, Chester O. Tucker, George Halpainen and Henry Tadberg from Eagle Harbor and Thomas H. McCormick, John Mc-Donald, John C. Alfsen, Fred C. Soliman, Paul Liedtke, Collin L. Westrope, David M. Small and Oscar Marshall from Portage Ship Canal, Hancock, Michigan.

THE SELF-RIGHTING LIFE-BOAT UNDER SAIL.

Series of sketches on U. S. Life Saving Service by M. J. Burns, circa 1879, published in the old Harper's Weeklies.

48

THE BREECHES BUOY.

BURNING A SIGNAL.

SURFMAN WITH LIFE-BELT.

LAUNCHING THE SURF-BOAT.

Captain Oliver Pilon, Keeper, Station Two Rivers.

Frederick W. Anderson, Keeper of the Oswego Station from October 28, 1892 until after the merger of the U. S. Life Saving Service with the U. S. Revenue Cutter Service formed the U. S. Coast Guard. Photo was taken around 1912. (Copied from an old photograph by Robert Oliphant of Oswego.)

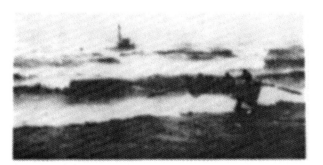

Life Saving crew going out to wreck of Francis Hinton, Two Rivers, Wisconsin, November 16, 1909.

Crew of Oswego Life Saving Station, Circa 1912.

Station Two Rivers, circa 1890.

Crew of Michigan City, Indiana Life Saving Station, Circa
1897. (Photo courtesy of Michigan City Historical Society,
Old Lighthouse Museum.)

Launching the surfboat, Michigan City, Indiana, 1906.
(Photo courtesy of the Michigan City Historical Society
and Old Lighthouse Museum.)

Crew of Ludington Life Saving Station hauls boat ashore
after rescue, 11 November 1940.

Surfboat drill during the summer months—station crews practiced capsizing and righting the surfboat so that they could readily right a boat in the event it was overturned in the sea. This picture shows the crew pulling the boat bottom-up.

Joseph Francis—Inventor of the Life Car.

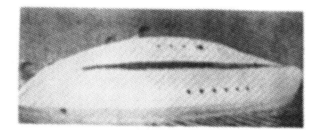

Surfboat drill—with the boat bottom-up, the crew would climb onto the bottom and right it by putting their weight on the righting lines that are attached to the gunwale.

Francis' patent corrugated galvanized iron life-car, invented 1838, perfected 1847. Successfully used on the coast of New Jersey, January 12th, 1850, saving 200 lives from the wreck of the ship Ayrshire, in a terrific snow storm.

Surfboat drill—the boat which had been capsized is now free of water and underway again. The complete drill was only a matter of seconds since the boat could be overturned and righted in less than one minute.

Francis Life Car in use.

U. S. Life Saving Service crew at Fairport Harbor, Ohio.
1909.

Old Chicago Life Saving Station, circa 1894.

56

A winter road leading into one of the Lake Superior stations. Those stations which were not fortunate enough to be located where roadways were plowed out had to resort to snowshoes and dog sleds as a means of transportation.

Breeches buoy rescue on the shores of Lake Superior.

A 36-foot "E" class powered lifeboat is readied by the crew for launching on rails from Old Chicago Life Saving Station, circa 1918. A full suit of sails and oars were kept in this lifeboat for emergencies.

Type "H" Motor Lifeboat under sail and power. The expanse of canvas was comparatively small but served to keep headway on the boat in case the motor gave out and help steady the boat in a seaway. On long runs, with favorable winds, the sail was used in conjunction with the motor to make the best speed.

The steamer George M. Cox stranded May 27, 1933 on a reef near Rock of Ages Light off the west end of Isle Royale in Lake Superior.

CHAPTER IV
THE STEAMBOAT INSPECTION SERVICE

The introduction in 1807 of Robert Fulton's steamboat *Clermont* signalled the beginning of a new era in American shipping. Interest in steam-powered navigation grew rapidly and in 1819, the *Savannah* became the first steam vessel to cross the Atlantic.

Unfortunately, these early steamboats were prone to disaster, with increasing numbers of persons losing their lives. By 1824, there had been so many fires, explosions and deaths that Congress directed the Secretary of the Treasury to conduct an investigation into the causes. Not until fourteen years later though, did Congress take any positive action. The Act of July 7, 1838 was the first step toward federal regulation of marine safety. Looking toward the "better security of the lives of passengers on board of vessels propelled in whole or in part by steam", the Act required owners or masters to employ a competent number of experienced engineers to operate their steam engines and to have their hulls inspected annually and the boilers every six months. Lifeboats, fire pumps and hose and signal lights were required and the owner or master had to obtain a license proving that he had complied with all the new regulations before he would be allowed to carry passengers.

District judges were given the responsibility of appointing "skilled and competent" persons to inspect the hulls and boilers. Inspectors were paid by the vessel owners at the rate of $5 for each boiler or hull inspected. If the vessel passed, a certificate of inspection was issued, which was required to be posted in a conspicuous place for the public information.

A final provision of the Act stated that any person who was employed on board a vessel, whose negligence, misconduct or dereliction to duty resulted in a loss of life, could be held accountable for the crime of manslaughter.

After the passage of the original Act (5 Stat. L., 304), modifications and extensions were voted into effect. Among these were the Act of March 3, 1843 (5 Stat. L., 626) which called for additional, emergency steering apparatus, the Act of February 22, 1847 (9 Stat. L., 127) which set a limit on the number of passengers which vessels regulated by the Act could carry, and the March 3, 1849 Act (9 Stat. L., 399) extended the limits to include all vessels bound from U. S. ports to any port in the Pacific or from any Pacific port to any U. S. Atlantic port.

August 30, 1852, Congress approved the "Steamboat Act" (10 Stat. L., 1852) which established the Steamboat Inspection Service. The President was authorized to appoint nine supervising inspectors who would meet once a year to set up rules and regulations for administering the inspection laws. These supervising inspectors were paid $1,500 per year, plus travel expenses. They were required to be "competent and experienced men in the construction and operation of merchant vessels". Each inspector had control and supervision of a specific geographic territory and was responsible for the supervision of local hull and boiler inspectors, assisting in actual inspections, reporting cases of neglect, carelessness, or inefficiency to the Secretary and to provide the Secretary with technical information relative to the welfare of the Service.

The Act also set up new regulations for the appointment and compensation of local inspectors in certain districts. In some cases, a commission made up of the Collector of Customs, the Supervising Inspector and the U. S. District Court Judge, would appoint two inspectors subject to final approval by the Secretary of the Treasury. Given the titles "Inspector of Hulls" and "Inspector of Boilers", these men were now paid a fixed salary, based on the amount of work required in their district. Fees for the inspectors were to be turned over to the Collector of Customs who submitted them to the U. S. Treasury. Local inspectors were now also empowered to act as a board for the licensing and classification of all engineers and pilots employed on board steamers which transported passengers.

Also included in the Steamboat Act were additional requirements for lifesaving equipment and fire prevention and a special license was established for vessels carrying dangerous or inflammable materials.

Initially, there was tremendous opposition to the new laws by vessel owners and masters, but their hostility was tempered as the benefits achieved by these regulations became more apparent. By 1862, attitudes had, for the most part, changed and as stated in the Service's annual report for that year, ". . . the cause of almost every accident to passenger steamers which now occurs can be readily traced to a violation of its provisions, or of the regulations of this board made pursuant thereto."

As good intentioned and effective as the Steamboat Act was, it contained one serious flaw, similar to that experienced in the beginning period of the Life Saving Service—there was no central authority in charge. The seriousness of this lack of centralized control was reported to the Secretary of the Treasury in the report of a special agent dated November 6, 1855. According to the agent, "A body without a head is a monster; and so likewise is a body with nine heads. With the Union divided into nine districts, and the supervising inspector in each district exercising a wide discretion in regard to rules and regulations, there has been no uniformity in the operation of the act."

The Chief of the Steamboat Inspection Division drew up a proposal for reorganizing the Service, which the Secretary of the Treasury presented to Congress in 1870 and which resulted in the Act of February 28, 1871 (16 Stat. L., 440). An administrative head, titled the "Supervising Inspector-General" was created who would have authority over the entire operation of the Service and be appointed by the President, approved by the Senate and under the Secretary of the Treasury. He received a salary of $3,500 plus ten cents a mile. Practically all previous legislation pertaining to inspection, licensing, passengers and cargo of steam-powered vessels was superseded or repealed by this Act. One important aspect of the legislation was that it extended to officers and crews of steam vessels, the same rights to protection previously afforded only to passengers. It also extended the authority of the law, applying it to "All steam vessels navigating any waters of the United States which are common highways of commerce, or open to general or competitive navigation, excepting public vessels of the United States, vessels of other countries, and boats propelled in whole or in part by steam for navigating canals."

Between 1872 and 1903, Congress passed numerous laws intended to make the Service more efficient. The "Passenger Act of 1882" (22 Stat. L., 186) authorized collectors of customs to direct that vessels be examined to determine the number of passengers they could safely transport, and the provisions for passenger safety. Foreign vessels carrying passengers were brought under the laws by the Act of August 7, 1882 (22 Stat. L., 346) and sixteen "special inspectors of foreign steam-vessels" were authorized. The *Revised International Rules and Regulations for Preventing Collisions at Sea* were adopted for all U. S.

vessels operating on the high seas or coastal waters on March 3, 1885 (23 Stat. L., 438). Inspection of boiler plates at the mills where they were manufactured was authorized January 22, 1894 (28 Stat. L., 28). On March 1, 1895 (28 Stat. L., 699) the sixteen foreign vessel inspector posts were abolished and their duties taken over by the local inspectors. The Steamboat-Inspection Service was placed under the classified Civil Service by Executive Order on March 2, 1896. Inspection requirements were extended January 18, 1897 (29 Stat. L., 489) to include all vessels propelled by gas, fluid, naptha or electric motors.

As pointed out earlier in this work, the Secretary of the Navy made a vigorous attempt between 1882 and 1885 to bring several departments under his authority. The Steamboat-Inspection Service was one of these. A more favorable proposal, however, was introduced December 4, 1901. This proposal became the law which created the Department of Commerce and Labor and on February 14, 1903 (32 Stat. L., 825), the Steamboat-Inspection Service left the Treasury Department and became a part of the new department.

Scandal rocked the Service in 1904 when on June 15th, the excursion steamer *General Slocum* caught fire on New York's East River and 957 persons, mostly women and children, perished. Eight days later, President Roosevelt appointed a commission to investigate and their report submitted October 8th placed the responsibility for the disaster on the Steamboat-Inspection Service. The report cited four major reasons for the Service's inadequacy: (1) too few inspectors were stationed in New York; (2) the public often opposed delays caused by reinspections; (3) owners were reluctant to keep lifesaving and firefighting equipment in an adequate condition; and (4) inadequate supervision. All officers connected with the disaster were ordered dismissed by the President.

The Act of March 3, 1905 (33 Stat. L., 1022) beefed up the Service's authority. Inspectors were authorized to prescribe to owners of vessels, the measures to be taken to prevent and/or extinguish fires and to establish regulations concerning the number and type of lifesaving equipment required. An executive committee made up of the Supervising Inspector-General and any two supervising inspectors was established. This committee could be called into session by the Secretary of Commerce and Labor at any time and with his approval was enpowered to "alter, amend, add to, or repeal any of the rules and regulations made by the board of supervising inspectors...".

A number of acts were passed between 1906 and 1913 which greatly increased the scope of the Service and assigned it new responsibilities. Most important among these was the "Motor-Boat Act", passed June 9, 1910 (36 Stat. L., 462). As defined by the Act, motorboats were all vessels, except tugs, which were propelled by machinery and were less than sixty-five feet in length. Steam-powered motorboats over forty feet were made subject to inspection, regulations were established calling for a licensed operator in all motor-boats carrying passengers and required that one life preserver be on board for each passenger carried. Lighting regulations and rules governing whistles, fog horns and bells also were set forth in the Act.

Congress on March 4, 1913 (37 Stat. L., 736) created the Department of Labor and the Steamboat-Inspection Service became a bureau of the remaining Department of Commerce. Other legislation followed and on March 4, 1915, the "Seamen's Act" (38 Stat. L., 1164) was passed and authorized local inspectors to examine applicants and grant certificates of service to able seamen and persons qualified to serve as lifeboatmen.

The duties of the Steamboat-Inspection Service as described in 1911 by the Supervising Inspector-General in his annual report were:

1. Inspection of vessels—their construction and equipment;
2. Examination and licensing of marine officers;
3. Examination and certification of seamen and lifeboatmen;
4. Determination of necessary complement of officers and crew and accommodations;
5. Conduct of investigations of marine casualties and violations of inspection laws;
6. Establishment of regulations to prevent collisions;
7. Regulation of the transportation of passengers and merchandise.

Two Steamboat-Inspection Service Districts were located in the Great Lakes region. The Eighth District included "all the waters of the Great Lakes north and west of Lake Erie, with their tributaries", while the Ninth District embraced "all the waters of the River St. Lawrence, Lakes Erie, Ontario, and Champlain, and their tributaries". Headquarters for the Eighth District were at Detroit with local inspectors being stationed in Detroit, Grand Haven, Marquette and Port Huron, Michigan; Chicago, Illinois; Milwaukee, Wisconsin; and Duluth, Minnesota. Cleveland, Ohio was headquarters for the Ninth District with inspectors in Cleveland and Toledo, Ohio; Buffalo and Oswego, New York; and Burlington, Vermont.

THE YEARS OF CONSOLIDATION
(1915-1946)
THE COAST GUARD IS BORN

America's emergence into the Twentieth Century included a period known as the "Progressive Era" during which there was a constant public outcry for an end to corruption and political waste. The progressives sought to reform the mechanics of political organization and urged on by muckraking journalists, all facets of government were brought under closer scrutiny.

An editorial in the Washington, D.C. *Evening Star* of April 5, 1912 called for the application of business principles to government agencies, decrying the apparent waste caused by duplication and dispersion of duties. A classic example of just such waste involved several agencies concerned with maritime safety. The Lighthouse Service, Steamboat-Inspection Service and Bureau of Navigation were units of the Department of Commerce and Labor, while collectors of customs, the Life Saving Service and Revenue Cutter Service operated under the Department of the Treasury, yet all had duties which were interrelated and in many cases, identical to those of the other services.

President William Howard Taft, a staunch proponent of consolidation and organization, appointed a "President's Commission on Economy and Efficiency", headed by the Honorable F. A. Cleveland. Although the Cleveland Commission did bring about numerous changes which greatly enhanced the efficiency of government, when it came to the maritime services, it became a victim of its own shortsightedness. Throughout its recommendations, the Commission stressed the doctrine of "unifunctionalism", one service for one job. The folly of such thinking was pointed out by Captain Commandant of the Revenue Cutter Service, Ellsworth P. Bertholf, whose arguments in defense of his Service's varied duties stated, "While none of these . . . individually requires constant attention, all of them are of such a coordinate nature as to permit them to be accomplished satisfactorily by one organization."

At any rate, the Cleveland Commission submitted its report to the President recommending the merger of the Lighthouse Service with the Life Saving Service and the abolishment of the Revenue Cutter Service. A second proposal was submitted by Secretary of Commerce and Labor, Charles Nagel, which called for the consolidation of the three services under his department.

Secretary of the Treasury, Franklin McVeigh, however, had a third alternative. He proposed the merger of the Revenue Cutter Service with the Life Saving Service and was so confident of its logic that he appointed Sumner Kimball, Superintendent of the Life Saving Service and Captain Commandant Bertholf to draw up a bill to that effect. McVeigh's argument that the rescue functions of the two services could compliment each other was amplified by the combined operations of the Ditch Plains Life Saving Station and the cutters MOHAWK and ACUSHNET during the dramatic rescue of the crew of the *Ontario*, afire off Montauk Point, April 8, 1912.

Secretary McVeigh's proposal was introduced to the Senate June 5, 1912 as S#2337 by Senator Charles E. Townsend of the Great Lakes state of Michigan, but received no real action until the Taft administration went out of power. Hearings on the merger were held in early 1914 and drawing strong support from both parties, the bill was approved by the Senate in March.

Ellsworth P. Bertholf

That December, President Wilson lent his support to the proposal, writing to Oscar W. Underwood, the House Democratic Leader that,

"It is of the highest consequence for the efficiency of both services that this bill should pass...".

Representative William C. Adamson of Georgia guided the bill through the House, stressing as one main point that the cuttermen would provide a trained Naval Reserve when needed. With World War I already sweeping across Europe, the point was a good one. The bill passed easily, 212-79 and on January 28, 1915, President Wilson signed it into law (28 Stat. L., 800).

Thus, 125 years after Alexander Hamilton received authorization for a fleet of cutters, the United States Coast Guard was born.

Under the Act, the Coast Guard was to become a part of the Navy when directed by the President and a board of cutter officers was appointed to meet with representatives of the Navy Department to draw up plans for the implementation of this provision. A second board was also appointed to establish the organization, operational and administrative patterns to be followed by the new service. Composed of former district superintendents of the Life Saving Service and cutter officers, the board compiled the initial guidelines into *Regulations, U. S. Coast Guard*.

Reorganization was no easy matter. On January 30, 1915, there were about 255 officers (including thirteen former district superintendents), 3,900 enlisted men and warrant officers, seventeen regions, four depots, an academy, twenty-five cruising cutters, twenty harbor cutters and 280 lifeboat stations in the Coast Guard. Since the new service was a branch of the military, existing classifications were used and under these classifications, district superintendents became commissioned officers, keepers became warrant officers, Number 1 Surfmen were made petty officers and the remaining surfmen were considered regular enlisteds. Discipline, longevity pay, uniform allowances and a retirement system were now applicable to everyone in the Service.

Captain Commandant Bertholf became the first Captain Commandant of the Coast Guard and the sole executive head, while Kimball was retired after forty-five years of service. He was authorized to receive three-fourths of his pay by special order of the President in recognition of his contribution to the country.

The Field Service of the Coast Guard was divided into twenty-four administrative units, with the Great Lakes cutters being assigned to Division VI and the lifesaving stations remaining Divisions, IX, X and XII. This organization was in effect for barely two years when the Coast Guard was temporarily transferred to the Navy for the duration of the First World War.

In 1920, the organization structure of the Coast Guard was again revised with the Field Service being divided into three major groups: Cruising, Patrol, and Lifesaving.

The Cruising Service contained seven divisions and the Bering Sea Patrol. On all the Great Lakes except Lake Ontario, the 5th Cruising Service Division, headquartered at Sault Ste. Marie (Michigan), was responsible for rendering assistance to vessels in distress and enforcement of maritime laws. Lake Ontario and the St. Lawrence River were under the supervision of the 2nd Division in New York.

One second-class cruising cutter, the KANKAKEE, the harbor cutter CHIPPEWA, the AB-1 (formerly *Advance*), AB-12 (formerly *Search*), AB-13 (formerly *Sentinel*), AB-17 (formerly *Vigilant*), AB-18 (formerly *Voyager*), patrol boats COOK and CRAWFORD and several picket boats were assigned to the Lakes Division.

Concerned primarily with deep-sea cruising, the second major group of the Field Service did not involve any units on the Great Lakes.

Lifesaving, the third major group, was, in essence, the same as the old Lifesaving Service. Buffalo, New York was headquarters for the Ninth District, which included twenty stations along the coasts of Lakes Ontario, Erie, and Huron (to Hammond's Bay). The Tenth District was comprised of twenty-one stations along Lake Huron west of Hammond Bay; the east coast of Lake Michigan, Beaver and Mackinac Island and Louisville, Kentucky. Its headquarters were at Grand Haven, Michigan. Lake Michigan's western coast and Lake Superior came under the Eleventh District, which consisted of twenty-two stations and was headquartered at Green Bay, Wisconsin.

The sixty-three lifesaving stations along the Great Lakes were: Big Sandy, Oswego, Charlotte, Niagara and Buffalo, New York; Erie, Pennsylvania; Ashtabula, Fairport, Cleveland, Lorain, and Marblehead, Ohio; Lake View Beach, Harbor Beach, Point Aux Barques, Port Austin, Tawas, Sturgeon Point, Thunder Bay Island, Middle Island and Hammond Bay, Michigan; in the Ninth District: Bois Blanc, Mackinac Island, Beaver Island, Charlevoix, North Manitou, South Manitou, Sleeping Bear Point, Point Betsie, Frankfort, Manistee, Big Sable Point, Ludington, Pentwater, White River, Muskegon, Grand Haven, Holland, South Haven and St. Joseph, Michigan; Michigan City, Indiana and Louisville, Kentucky in the Tenth District; and South Chicago, Jackson Park, Old Chicago, and Evanston, Illinois; Kenosha, Racine, Milwaukee, Sheboygan, Two Rivers, Kewaunee, Sturgeon Bay Canal, Bailey Harbor and Plum Island, Wisconsin; White Fish Point, Vermillion, Two Heart River, Deer Park, Grand Marais, Marquette, Eagle Harbor and Portage, Michigan; and Duluth and North Superior, Minnesota in the Eleventh District.

Recruiting offices were located at Chicago and Cleveland under the supervision of a warrant officer. Sub-units were also operating in some of the other cities along the Lakes.

The officer-in-charge of the Harbor Beach, Michigan, station also enforced the regulations governing use of that port as a harbor of refuge. Captain of the Port offices were opened in Chicago Harbor and along the St. Mary's River at Sault Ste. Marie, Michigan.

On January 17, 1920, Congress passed the Volstead Act and for the next fourteen years, the Coast Guard would be charged with the responsibility of ensuring that no illicit liquor entered the country through its seacoasts, including the Great Lakes. Defiance of prohibition had grown to such proportions by 1924 that Congress appropriated $13,853,980 to expand the Coast Guard. Smuggling on the Great Lakes reached its peak between the fall of 1927 and the spring of 1928. Station crews were doubled, the number of patrol boats was increased to twenty and seventy-five picket boats were added to increase the Service's effectiveness. A machine shop was established at Buffalo to overhaul the engines and keep the boats running and a radio station was established at Buffalo. In 1930, Canada passed the King Resolution which greatly reduced the amount of smuggling from Canada and on December 5, 1933, the Twenty-First Amendment was ratified, ending prohibition.

By 1935, the administration of the Coast Guard had again been reorganized into four Areas, each commanded by a Captain. These Areas were subdivided into Divisions and Districts. Great Lakes operations came under the Northern Area which was divided into the Cleveland and Chicago Divisions. Thirteen stations were assigned to the Ninth District with Headquarters at Buffalo, New York; twenty-eight were within the Tenth District, headquartered at Grand Haven; and twenty-four came under the Green Bay, Wisconsin-based Eleventh District. The Ninth District was in the Cleveland Division while the Tenth and Eleventh Districts were in the Chicago Division.

Prior to the 1930's, domestic icebreaking had not been a primary concern of either the public or the Coast Guard. Year 'round navigation of the Great Lakes was not even dreamed about, their annual closing being accepted as a fact of life. Most of the cities were connected by the railways and it didn't matter a great deal that the Lakes were frozen over. In the thirties, however, this began to change, due mostly to the increasing use of oil rather than coal. Simple economics dictated that large storehouses of oil could not be maintained, nor could railway tank cars satisfy a community's thirst for oil. Thus, oil barges became the principle means of transporting the precious fuel and it became a necessity to keep the waterways open.

In 1932, a new class of cutter, designed to have icebreaking capabilities was constructed. The first of this new class was built at the DeFoe Works, Bay City, Michigan. She was 165 feet in length with a steel-strengthened hull and powered by a 1,500 h.p. steam turbine. Christened the Coast Guard Cutter ESCANABA, she was launched September 17, 1932 and accepted by the Service November 23rd. Assigned to the homeport of Grand Haven, Michigan, ESCANABA sailed into her new home December 9, 1932 in the midst of a blizzard. Twenty

Sketch of U. S. Coast Guard Cutter ESCANABA by Larry Van Alstyne.

days later, she made her first rescue, picking up two pilots who had crashed on Lake Michigan. The rescue received a great deal of notoriety since the ESCANABA had located the survivors clinging to the plane's wing in the dead of night on a storm-tossed sea. No easy feat.

One of the most notable rescues involving the ESCANABA took place during one of those infamous November gales, in 1934. The whaleback steamer *Henry W. Cort* bound for Chicago had been caught by surprise when the wind shifted directions and increased to gale force. About 8:30 in the evening of November 30, 1934, the *Cort* began her run for the safety of Muskegon, Michigan. She was going in at full speed, when the monstrous seas lifted her up and smashed her into the north breakwater.

The lookout at Muskegon Coast Guard Station had seen the *Cort's* plight and a power surfboat had been launched. Chief Boatswain's Mate John Basch lashed himself to the wheel as the surfboat was tossed about by the swirling seas. The angry waters smashed the rudder and nearly swamped the boat, washing Jack Dipert over the side. Unable to help the *Cort*, the crew of the surfboat now had to fight for its own survival. After nearly two hours, the remaining crewmen were ashore, but there was no sign of young Dipert.

Twelve miles further south, the Grand Haven Station had likewise launched a boat, receiving word of the disaster about 10:00 p.m. It took the Grand Haven boat over an hour to cover the distance to Muskegon, almost capsizing along the way. Chief Boatswain's Mate William A. Preston brought his boat close enough to the *Cort* to reassure himself that the crew was safe and then, deciding that nothing could be done at that point, proceeded to Muskegon to join forces with Basch. Throughout the late evening, rescuers continued to arrive. About 11:50 p.m., the ESCANABA left Grand Haven to join the effort, experiencing a particularly rough journey. It was decided that a human chain would edge its way out onto the breakwater and bring the survivors ashore via the breeches buoy. Lashed together by a long line, the lifesavers made their way along the icy rocks amid smashing waves and stinging sleet. It took an hour to reach the end of the breakwater. A line was tossed to the *Cort*, now less than fifty feet away. Four hours later, the rescuers and twenty-five survivors reached shore. Both Preston's boat

and the ESCANABA had been standing by ready to assist if needed. Not a single man had been lost, except for surfman Jack Dipert of Muskegon.

The idea of a Coast Guard air capability had originally been promoted by 2nd Lieutenant Norman B. Hall and 3rd Lieutenant Elmer F. Stone, two officers aboard the cutter ONODAGA, who envisioned it as a means of more efficiently searching the sea lanes for derelict vessels. The idea received approval from Captain B. M. Chiswell, their commanding officer, and Coast Guard Headquarters appointed Captain Charles A. McAllister, the Service's Chief Engineer, to draft a proposal. The Navy Department agreed to accept two Coast Guard officers for pilot training and McAllister's plan was submitted to Congress as part of the Naval Appropriation Act of 1916. Signed into law on August 29th, the Act provided for establishment of ten Coast Guard Air Stations along the coasts, including those of the Great Lakes, an aviation school and a corps of fifteen officers and forty enlisted men. Unfortunately, no funds for implementing the program were granted and no further action was taken until 1920.

Coast Guard pilots continued to be trained by the Navy, many serving in France during World War I. Following the war, in May 1919, three Navy flying boats, the NC-1, -3 and -4 began a transatlantic flight to prove the value of a patrol plane capable of landing on water. Only one, the NC-4 completed the journey, but co-piloting that plane was Lt. Elmer F. Stone, a Coast Guard officer. The flight had made its point and in 1920, Commandant William R. Reynolds secured six Curtiss HS-2L flying boats on loan from the Navy to establish an experimental air station at Morehead City, North Carolina. The station closed after fifteen months due to a lack of operating funds.

Prohibition enforcement brought about the next movement toward a Coast Guard air wing with a Vought UO-1 seaplane operating out of Squantum, Massachusetts Naval Reserve Air Station in early 1925. The plane later moved to Gloucester Harbor and in 1926, a second station opened at Cape May, New Jersey.

During the 1930's, air stations were operated at Salem, Massachusetts; Cape May; San Diego, California; Port Angeles, Washington; Biloxi, Mississippi; and Miami and St. Petersburg, Florida. In addition, Air Patrol Detachments were assigned to San Antonio, Texas and

Charleston, South Carolina. There had been plans to use an Air Patrol Detachment at Buffalo, New York, but due to a lack of sufficient aircraft and inadequate funding, these plans were scrapped.

In 1938, a Grumman V-118 twin-engine amphibian was assigned to the Great Lakes Air Patrol Detachment established at Traverse City, Michigan. Commanded by Lt. A. E. Harned, the detachment was to operate for three months to determine the feasibility of constructing an Air Station there. It was determined to continue operating the Detachment on a seasonal basis only.

On December 15th, 1932, the Coast Guard inaugurated a series of conferences on Great Lakes Communications. Attending the conference were representatives of shipping companies, radio companies, the U. S. Coast Guard and the Canadian Ministry of Marine. At this first "Great Lakes Distress Conference", the primary concern was devising means to improve response to distress calls. The Coast Guard was requested to coordinate distress communications and Captain H. H. Wolf, Commander Northern Area, drew up a proposed *Great Lakes Area Distress Coordination Plan*. A second conference was held at Toronto, Canada on May 7, 1933 to analyze the plan and discuss ways to provide for greater safety. These conferences were held annually after 1933 and the convening sites alternated between U. S. and Canadian cities. Many problems relating to radio communications were ironed out by these conferences.

The International Convention for Safety of Life at Sea, in May 1929, drafted the *Safety of Life at Sea Treaty* which set forth certain radio requirements for vessels making international voyages, but the Great Lakes were not included since they were "inland seas" completely between the U. S. and Canada. This treaty, however, would not become law in the United States until November 1936, and during its debates on appropriate legislation, Congress decided to apply the same rules to vessels on the Great Lakes. This brought a strong and rapid protest from shipping interests on the Lakes; thus when the Communications Act of 1934 was passed, it did not include the Great Lakes. Instead, it directed the Federal Communications Commission (FCC) to conduct a "Great Lakes Radio Survey" to determine the radio requirements necessary or desirable for

ships navigating these inland seas. On October 17, 1938, representatives of the Coast Guard met with members of the U. S. and Canadian Radio Commissions at Ottawa and many items for a proposed treaty were tentatively agreed upon. Three years later, a "Technical Subcommittee Considering Great Lakes Radio Agreement with Canada was formed by the State Department under chairmanship of E. M. Webster of the FCC, a former Coast Guard officer who had been a delegate to London in 1929 and who was largely responsible for the ensuing U. S. legislation. The subcommittee drafted a proposed treaty, which called for all passenger and cargo ships of 100 gross tons and above, belonging to either country navigating the Great Lakes, to carry radio equipment capable of transmitting on 2182 kc at least fifty statute miles for passenger vessels; thirty-five statute miles by cargo vessels of 1,000 gross tons and over; and at least twenty-five statute miles by cargo vessels less than 1,000 gross tons. Any further action on a treaty though, was delayed until the end of World War II.

Progress was being made in the field of aids to navigation also and the period between the world wars brought many changes. An airways division was added to the Lighthouse Service on October 1, 1926. Headed by a chief engineer, this division examined the airways and emergency landing fields and erected and maintained aids to air navigation. Existing facilities were used as much as possible until 1933 when the division was transferred to the Assistant Secretary for Aeronautics, Department of Commerce.

Electronics was rapidly changing the complexion of the Service. Many lights had become automated; radio fog signals had been introduced on the Great Lakes in June 1925 by the Huron Lightship; automatic time clocks were operating the electric range lights and telephone service connected even the most remote light stations. Local notices to mariners for the Great Lakes were published, using a new system, at Detroit beginning March 2, 1928. Mobile radiobeacons were extensively tested on Lake Michigan during 1933 and achieved favorable results. The following year tests of second and third class nun buoys were experimentally left on stations in the Great Lakes to determine the feasibility of not removing the buoys during the winter. Over eighty buoys were tested and found to have suffered only negligible damage from running ice.

By the end of 1934, the Pintsch type gas buoys had been converted to use the newer acetylene gas. Where before, the gas had to be pumped into the shell of the buoy, the acetylene was contained in portable containers called accumulators. This system permitted the use of quick flashing lights, which made a better characteristic, and it also greatly facilitated the recharging of the buoys with gas, since the portable gas cylinders could be placed in the buoys without the use of large vessels.

The Huron Lightship was moved to the left, or west side of the upbound channel about six miles north of the mouth of the Upper St. Clair River on Lake Huron. It was felt the move would provide both a better aid to navigation and a better anchorage for the lightship. In order to conform with the lateral system of buoyage, the vessel was painted black, making it the only black lightship in use in the United States.

Also in 1936, a battery-powered electric solenoid-operated fog bell striker of the clapper type was experimentally installed at the Peshtigo Reef Light Station on Lake Michigan and an agreement was reached between U. S. and Canadian lighthouse administrations adopting identical principles of radio beacon operation.

Notices to mariners regarding Great Lakes aids to navigation began being broadcast by radiotelephone from Sault Ste. Marie in 1937. The station also broadcast weather forecasts, ice conditions, and information on wrecks and derelicts. Within a year this program was expanded to five other radiophone broadcasting stations on the Great Lakes.

Another important development in 1937 was the automation of the ST. CLAIR Lightship, making it "like no other lightship in the entire world". Practically all the equipment on the ST. CLAIR was installed in duplicate so that when any malfunction occurred, a second mechanism could be switched on to replace it. Radiotelephone signals from the vessel kept its operator, eight miles away, aware of any problems. The light was completely automatic, being turned on and off by an astronomical clock. During foul weather, the shore operator could override the automatic systems and activate the vessel's light, radio beacon and fog

Coast Guardsman standing on plank on broken ice at side of a lighted buoy as he fastens lines from boom which will raise the heavy buoy to the deck of the buoy tender. Taken on Western Lake Erie, 10 December 1942.

horn. In order to let the operator know for certain that he had indeed activated the fog horn, a remarkable system was devised. A microphone was arranged so that when the signal was functioning properly, the radio beacon would sound its signal the full sixty seconds of each minute. If, however, the fog horn did not work correctly, the microphone would automatically shut off the radio beacon for five seconds each minute. Once aware of the horn's malfunction, the operator needed only to press a button to activate the duplicate horn. A similar system also was installed at the Peshtigo Reef Lighthouse in Green Bay. The light was controlled from Sherwood Point, nine miles away.

As the Lighthouse Service became more technical in its operation and its equipment achieved greater sophistication and complexity, the requirements for broader educational backgrounds among its keepers were necessarily increased. The higher levels required coupled with the trend away from isolated living resulted in increasing problems in the recruitment of young men to be assistant keepers. At the same time, the experienced old timers began retiring and the Service was facing manpower shortages.

In 1938, President Roosevelt directed the Coast Guard and the Lighthouse Service to make a study into how the two could be best combined to produce governmental economies. The result was the President's Reorganization Plan No. 11 which became effective July 1, 1939. Under this plan the Lighthouse Service was absorbed by the Coast Guard with all vessel personnel and members of the field services offered the choice of either retaining their civilian status or transferring to a military rank or rating.

When the Lighthouse Service merged with the Coast Guard, there were over two thousand aids to navigation in service on the Great Lakes, maintained by ten lighthouse tenders. There also were forty-five radio beacon stations and six stations broadcasting weather and notices to mariners in operation. Fifty-eight Coast Guard stations, fifteen with radio-telephone transmitters, numerous small boats and the cutters ESCANABA and TAHOMA were also serving along the Lake shores. In addition, the U. S. Weather Bureau had seventy-six observation stations located there.

The seventeen districts of the Lighthouse Service, together with the nine divisions and thirteen districts of the Coast Guard, were consolidated into thirteen Coast Guard districts. District Commanders were analogous to the old division commanders and were provided a staff of specialists, including those who had been district commanders under the old system. The Great Lakes became the Ninth Coast Guard District under command of Captain H. G. Fisher.

Coast Guard Cutter SENECA stationed on the Great Lakes prior to World War II.

1939 also saw the creation, by Congress, of the United States Coast Guard Reserve (Civilian). An organization of yacht and motorboat owners, it was created as a civilian affiliate of the Coast Guard to assist in the boating safety education of the public. This unique group soon proved its worth on the Great Lakes. Lieutenant Commander R. E. Wood, Director of the Coast Guard Reserve for the Cleveland

Maumee Bay Range Light seen through the direction finding loop of the U. S. Coast Guard Cutter CROCUS.

District, devised a system for providing improved weather forecasts to boaters. As part of the Reserve's program to improve the safety and pleasure of boating, Wood's plan called for weather broadcasts giving forecasts for specific areas, small craft warnings and storm information. Fifteen stations began operating May 15, 1940 and several others were soon added so that the entire Lakes area received coverage, providing mariners with up-to-date and localized weather information.

War came to Europe September 1, 1939 when

Hitler's troops marched into Poland. President Roosevelt proclaimed a National Emergency a week later and the Coast Guard prepared for war. On September 18th, an Executive Order authorized the addition of 4,500 personnel and directed the increase, repair, enlargement and equipping of Coast Guard facilities. Captains of the Ports were directed to furnish a daily report of the movement of all foreign merchant vessels and aircraft. This was later expanded to include domestic cargo vessels, passenger vessels, tugs, barges and bay, sound, or river vessels.

As the inevitable entry of the United States into the war drew closer, other proclamations, acts and Executive Orders were issued, giving the Coast Guard greater responsibility as a "Federal Police" agency. On November 5, 1940, Captains of the Port were designated at twenty-nine "key ports" including Sault Ste. Marie and Detroit, Michigan; Cleveland, Ohio; Chicago, Illinois and Duluth, Minnesota. The primary duties of these new offices were to enforce the anchorage regulations and supervise the handling of explosives and dangerous cargoes. These ports were designated as "Headquarters Ports" on March 25, 1941 giving them jurisdiction over the coastal areas and subports within a geographic area extending from the adjacent COTP's. In addition to those ports already mentioned, Buffalo and Oswego, New York and Marquette, Michigan were designated as "Headquarters Ports".

February 19, 1941, the United States Coast Guard Auxiliary and Reserve Act established the Reserve as a military component of the Coast Guard and re-designated the civilian affiliate as the Auxiliary. Reservists were divided into regulars and temporaries with the regulars serving full-time with pay and the temporaries further subdivided into six categories receiving no military pay.

On November 1st, the Coast Guard became part of the Navy and December 8th, war was declared on Japan, followed by a similar declaration against Italy and Germany on the 11th.

Port Security became an important responsibility of the Coast Guard during the war, and a principle one on the Great Lakes. COTP's were designated at twenty ports in the two districts comprising the Great Lakes portion of the Ninth Naval District. The District Commanders were retitled as the District Coast Guard Officer. The Ninth District was sub-divided into three geographical areas, headquartered at Cleveland, Chicago, and St. Louis. We will concern ourselves only with the Cleveland and Chicago divisions.

The Great Lakes were an important wartime waterway and shipbuilding in the region attained large proportions, making sabotage a principal threat. It was essential to keep the iron ore moving to the steel production centers and the grain, coal, petroleum and other war-related products safely flowing to their destinations. Regulars, regular Reservists and Temporary Reservists were charged with guarding the lake shore, docks, vessels, bridges, patrolling the harbors, manning lookouts and keeping the lake traffic safely moving. To ensure the protection and security of Lake vessels, armed guards were provided by the Coast Guard. This drain on Coast Guard manpower was later relieved somewhat by the commissioning of licensed officers of the Lake Carriers as Temporary Reserve officers.

Although Port Security had gained new importance as a Coast Guard mission, the more traditional roles continued as major responsibilities. Maintenance of the Great Lakes' aids to navigation remained substantially the same as it had been prior to the war. During 1941, two new light stations were completed and construction begun on a new lifeboat station on Lake St. Clair. Both of the new lighthouses were offshore, remote controlled stations. One replaced the Lake St. Clair lightship and the other was located at Gravelly Shoal in Saginaw Bay. The lifeboat station, on Belle Isle in Detroit, was completed in 1942 and its mooring basin, launchway and boat handling facilities were considered to be the finest procurable.

Ice, the traditional nemesis of Great Lakes navigation, began receiving new attention as tentative plans were made to construct a heavy-duty icebreaker which would enable the Coast Guard to keep important channels open until later in the fall and reopen navigation at an earlier date each spring. The new cutter would have a seventy-four foot beam, making it wider than any vessel in normal service on the Lakes and ensuring that sufficiently wide channels could be broken. December 17, 1941, the Third Supplemental National Defense Appropriation Act approved $8,000,000 for construction of an icebreaker with a displacement of 5,000 tons, a length of 290 feet and engines of 10,000 shaft horsepower. The Toledo Shipbuilding Company was awarded the contract. On March 20, 1943 her keel was laid. Almost a year later, March 4, 1944 she was launched and December 20th commissioned, the U. S. Coast Guard Cutter MACKINAW. New Year's Eve she arrived at Cheboygan, Michigan, commanded by Commander C. H. Stober. At the time of her launching, MACKINAW was the most powerful, most modern, and most capable icebreaker in the world for her designed purposes.

Public Law 773, passed by the 77th Congress and signed by President Roosevelt on November 23, 1942 amended the Coast Guard Auxiliary and Reserve Act of 1941 to provide for the establishment of a Women's Reserve. Lieutenant Commander Dorothy C. Stratton was appointed to serve as Director of the Women's Reserve. It was she who coined the acronym, SPAR, which became the familiar name for the Women's Reserve. She derived SPAR from the first letters of the Coast Guard's Latin motto and English translation:—"Semper Paratus, Always Ready". The father of Captain Mildred McAfee, Director of the Waves, pointed out that the letters also represent the Four Freedoms: Speech, Press, Assembly, and Religion.

The primary objective of the Spars was to replace Coast Guardsmen who were filling shore billets, enabling them to be assigned to sea. A total of fifteen officers and 153 enlisted women comprised the initial complement of Spars, having transferred from the Navy. To these were added 378 enlisted and 106 officers who were recruited directly within two months of the Spars' creation.

On February 21, 1943, the first eight Spars arrived in the Ninth Naval District (Cleveland). For a while recruiting was the primary duty of all women. Once a week they were called from their duties to go on recruiting trips. Three more arrived in March and were given training as pharmacist mate strikers at St. Luke's Hospital. In May, arrivals began to increase. On the 1st, eighteen storekeepers strikers reported aboard and on the 15th, twenty-six more arrived. By the end of 1943, Cleveland had 153 enlisted Spars, all in Cleveland except for a few on recruiting assignments. There were twenty-three officers in the district; six on recruiting duty, two in public relations, three in communications, one in civil engineering and one was assigned to the Hol-

lenden House, which the Spars and Waves were using as a barracks. Later, as the numbers of women increased, the quarters were moved to the Salvation Army's Evangeline Residence.

By June 1944 there were 398 enlisted Spars in the Ninth District, serving in mostly clerical or communications billets but with some exceptions. In November, the district boasted its first Spar Chief, a yeoman. The program reached its peak in August 1945 when 662 Spars were assigned throughout the District. While most were stationed at the Office of the District Coast Guard Officer in Cleveland, many were assigned to the bases at Buffalo, Detroit, Milwaukee, Chicago, and Sault Ste. Marie. Twenty served as recruiters, eight were assigned to Marine Hospitals and twelve were stationed at the Chesterland Radio Station.

Although initially, the men displayed a general lack of enthusiasm for their female replacements, their attitude improved as the program developed. Perhaps the best proof of their efficiency was Commodore J. A. Hirshfield's expression of regret when the end of the war brought the end of the Spar program. Hirshfield, the District Coast Guard Officer during the latter part of 1944 and the first District Commander when the service was returned to the Treasury Department, had often voiced his confidence in the Women's Reserve and frequently campaigned for their establishment as a permanent affiliate.

In June 1943 an event took place in the North Atlantic which carried grave significance for residents of the Great Lakes. The Cutter ESCANABA, which, until the war, had been homeported in Grand Haven, Michigan, was serving on convoy duty as part of Task Unit 24.8.2. Before departing Narsarssuak, Greenland, ESCANABA's crew had been startled to learn the Germans were predicting the doom of the transport ship USAT *Fairfax*, which the task force was escorting to St. John's, Newfoundland. Extra precautions were taken and after conducting a search for submarines with no result, the convoy left port at 10 p.m. on June 10, 1943. Encountering dense fog and many icebergs on the 12th, the convoy turned northwest to pass around the ice. Later that evening, Lieutenant Commander Carl Peterson, skipper of the ESCANABA, told his crew that those not on watch could remain in their bunks and try to catch up on some lost sleep.

With most of the crew sleeping in, only a

U. S. Coast Guard Cutter ESCANABA ready for war.

handful were on duty the morning of the third day. Seaman First Class Raymond O'Malley was the helmsman at 5:10 a.m. when "a noise which sounded like three or four bursts of 20mm machine gun fire was clearly heard in the pilot house". Peterson and his Executive Officer, Lieutenant Robert H. Prause, Jr., who had been asleep aft of the wheel house, immediately came up to the bridge. Within seconds, Prause was dead as a tremendous explosion ripped the vessel in two. She sank in less than three minutes. No explosion had been heard by the other escort vessels and no signals had been seen or heard. Observers on the Cutter STORIS, the nearest vessel to the ESCANABA when she sank, said a "cloud of dense black and yellow smoke billowed upwards into the air." Although the STORIS and the Cutter RARITAN arrived at the scene only ten minutes after the sinking, only two survivors could be found: the helmsman Raymond O'Malley and Boatswains Mate Second Class Melvin Baldwin.

No sufficiently conclusive evidence was ever found to explain what caused the ESCANABA's sinking. Probable explanations would be that her loss was due to a mine, torpedo or internal magazine and depth charge explosion. Remotely supporting the torpedo theory is the possibility that the machine-gun-like noises O'Malley heard just before the explosion, could have been caused by the hydrophone effect of a torpedo, heard through the loud speaker, which was connected and clearly audible in the pilot house.

On August 4, 1943, 20,000 people gathered at Grand Haven to pay tribute to the 101 officers and men who were lost when the ESCANABA went down. Her rigged mast, removed at Manitowoc in 1942 when she was converted to a warship, a lifeboat raft, and some other parts are all that remain of the proud cutter whose ten years of heroic exploits on the Great Lakes endeared her to all who knew her. On May 30, 1944 the mast and gear were erected at Kelly Memorial Park as a permanent testimonial to the ESCANABA and every year during the Coast Guard Festival, a memorial service is held there. To further demonstrate their love and appreciation of the cutter, the citizens of Grand Haven and its surrounding area purchased more than $1,000,000 in U. S. war bonds to build another cutter to proudly bear the name ESCANABA.

The ESCANABA was not the only Great Lakes casualty of war in the North Atlantic. Before the war, cutters had been assigned to weather-ship stations in mid-ocean to supply meteorological data for transoceanic ships and aircraft. This duty became increasingly important after war was declared since the convoy system and aircraft needed accurate weather data. As the larger cutters assumed more essential duties, 180-foot buoy tenders took over the responsibility for weather stations. They proved quite inefficient for the job though, and were soon replaced. Several Great Lakes freighters were converted into weather ships by the Coast Guard and assigned as replacements for the

Training for war at Grand Haven Recruit Training Center.

buoy tenders. Old, slow and practically defenseless, the former lake carriers were easy prey for submarines and one of them, the *Muskeget,* after serving only a few days on her station, disappeared without a trace. Originally named the *Cornish,* the lake freighter had been chartered by the Navy before she was turned over to the Coast Guard and comm'ssioned *Muskeget* in June 1942. Commanded by Lieutenant Commander C. E. Toft, she left Boston August 24, 1942, arriving on station, 450 miles south of Cape Farewell, Greenland, a week later. She was last heard from on September 8th while she awaited her relief ship, the *Monomoy.* No trace was ever found of the *Muskeget* and after a year, her nine officers, 107 enlisted men, four civilians, and one public health officer were declared officially dead.

Closer to home, one of the worst disasters in Great Lakes history took place at Cleveland. About 2:20 on the afternoon of October 20, 1944 an explosion of liquid gas rocked the storage tank area of the East Ohio Gas Company. The initial blast was followed by several smaller explosions and a tremendous fire. Before it was over, more than 150 persons had perished and hundreds of homes were completely destroyed. Property damage was estimated at $7,000,000. Although not the direct responsibility of the Coast Guard, the fire presented a serious threat to the entire waterfront area and all available Coast Guard personnel and equipment were mobilized. Local Temporary Reserve units, augmented by TR's from Fairport and Lorain reported to the Captain of the Port. In all, 453 Reservists assisted in preventing the fire's spread, policing the area, protecting merchants

from looting and recovering bodies. The Coast Guard was credited with preventing five tanks of highly noxious and explosive material at a nearby plant from exploding and keeping the fire from spreading. It took nearly three days of intensive effort before the danger passed and the Coast Guard could secure its activities.

The bulk of activity on the Great Lakes throughout the war was concerned with Captain of the Port and Harbor Patrol duties and after the issuance of Executive Order No. 9083 of February 28, 1942, Marine Inspection. The order had placed certain functions of the Bureau of Marine Inspection and Navigation under the Coast Guard. July 16, 1946, the transfer was made permanent.

Toward the end of 1944, the Lake Carriers Association asked the Coast Guard to examine the use of radar as a possible solution to certain Great Lakes shipping problems. During March, 1945, preliminary tests were made using equipment which had been installed aboard the MACKINAW. A coordinating committee consisting of representatives from the U. S. Coast Guard, the Federal Communications Commission, equipment manufacturers and the Lake Carriers Association was formed to correlate data and determine actions necessary to integrate the uses of radar into a complete system of electronic navigation. The Coast Guard, serving in an advisory capacity, offered technical and engineering assistance to the program.

The Coast Guard icebreaker MACKINAW framed in a windrowed ice field. The "BIG MAC" is at rest after breaking a path from the Sault Ste. Marie Locks to Lake Superior, through Whitefish Bay. Her cutaway bow crushes the ice as she pushes forward with all the might of 12,000 horsepower delivered from six engines.

CHANGING TIMES (1946-1976)

On January 1, 1946, the Coast Guard was returned to the Treasury Department and resumed its peacetime activities. The Great Lakes region was now the Ninth Coast Guard District under the command of Commodore James A. Hirshfield. The new District Commander had been one of only six Coast Guardsmen to receive the Navy Cross, the sea services' second highest award for valor. As skipper of the Coast Guard Cutter CAMPBELL, Hirshfield rammed his vessel into U-606, a German submarine which had earlier torpedoed three ships. Commodore Hirshfield came to the Ninth District in 1944 and bore the distinction of being the first flag rank officer to serve as the District Commander. He also would occupy the post longer than any of his successors, serving from 1944 until September, 1950. He later served as Assistant Commandant.

The Ninth District Commodore Hirshfield commanded, was essentially the same as it is today, stretching from Massena, New York to Duluth, Minnesota and encompassing a total shoreline of 5,480 miles. To patrol this vast area, the Coast Guard had, the newly designated traverse City Air Station; the icebreaking cutter, MACKINAW; the 180-foot buoy tenders, ACACIA, SUNDEW, TAHOMA, TUPELO, WOODBINE and WOODRUSH. (In December, 1947, the 180-foot MESQUITE was added to the Great Lakes fleet); several harbor tugs and fifty-one Coast Guard stations.

As the troops began returning home from post-war Europe, the Coast Guard began returning to its role as the protector of life and property on America's waterways. One of the most important missions, as always, was search and rescue (SAR). At the request of the Joint Chiefs of Staff, an Air-Sea Rescue Agency (ASR) had been established February 22, 1944. The Coast Guard Commandant was given responsibility for the direction of ASR but actual operations were conducted by the other branches of the service. When the Coast Guard returned to the Treasury Department in 1946, it assumed full responsibility for civilian search and rescue. For the next decade extensive planning and development by several agencies, both domestic and international, resulted in the formulation of international search and rescue agreements and a *National Search and Rescue Plan*. Under the National SAR Plan, adopted in March 1956, the Coast Guard was given the additional responsibility of organizing all avail-able SAR facilities into a single network. SAR coordinators were designated for the three SAR regions with the Commandant of the Coast Guard assuming responsibility for the Maritime Region. He further divided his responsibility into eleven sub-divisions. The U. S. portion of the Great Lakes and other navigable U. S. waters in the Ninth District became designated as the Cleveland Sub-Region and a Rescue Coordination Center (RCC) was established at the District Commander's Headquarters in Cleveland. The Cleveland RCC was, and is, responsible for coordinating all participating search and rescue units and facilities within the Ninth District.

Actual rescue operations, depending on the seriousness of the incident, were handled by local Coast Guard units and overseen by one of eleven Group Offices. Groups were comprised of all Coast Guard facilities in a given geographical area with the controlling facility designated as Group Command. The eleven Group Offices were located at: Buffalo, Cleveland, Detroit, Charlevoix, Ludington, Chicago, Two Rivers, Sault Ste. Marie, Portage, Duluth, and Hancock.

The air rescue capabilities of the Great Lakes Coast Guard were expanded in 1965 when $500,000 was appropriated for construction of a second air station at Detroit. Located at the Selfridge Air Force Base in Mount Clemons, Michigan, the new station was to be equipped with three gas-turbine amphibious helicopters. Officially known as the Sikorsky HH52A, these helicopters were designed to fly 190 miles, pick up an injured person either by using a rescue hoist or by landing on the water and return to base with a safe margin of fuel remaining. The Air Station officially opened in June 1966 under the command of Commander James W. Swanson. Original complement for the station was ten officers and twenty-nine enlisted men. During the period from July 1966 to July 1974, Air Station Detroit has been credited with saving three hundred and thirty lives.

By 1965, the Ninth District operated 160 floating and shore units. These included the Traverse City Air Station, the icebreaker MACKINAW, seven 180-foot buoy tenders, five smaller buoy tenders, HURON Lightship, five harbor tugs, fifty-one stations, eleven Group Offices, and eighty manned lights.

In his *Transportation Message to Congress* on March 2, 1966, President Lyndon B. Johnson proposed the establishment of a Department of Transportation (DOT) to coordinate federal programs and agencies involved in the promotion and control of transportation. Officially known as Public Law 89-670, the bill establishing the DOT became effective April 1, 1967. Alan Boyd, former Undersecretary for Transportation in the Department of Commerce was appointed to head the Department and the Federal Aviation Administration, Federal Highway Administration, Federal Railroad Administration, the Coast Guard and the St. Lawrence Seaway Corporation comprised the basic elements. Thus after nearly 177 years of association with the Department of the Treasury, the Coast Guard began a new era as an agency of the Department of Transportation.

For the next ten years, many changes would occur both in the physical make-up and the missions of the Service. A third Air Station was established at Glenview Naval Air Station in the Chicago area in 1969; older stations at Chicago, Racine, Sandusky, Munising, Grand Marais, Plum Island, Portage, Sodus Point, South Haven, Split Rock Light, and others were disestablished or turned over to the Coast Guard Auxiliary; new stations were built at St. Ignace, Michigan and Alexandria Bay, New York.

U. S. Coast Guard Cutter BRAMBLE in 1962.

The 1970 River and Harbor Act authorized a *Great Lakes-St. Lawrence Seaway Navigation Season Extension Demonstration Program.* Since then, the Coast Guard has played several key roles in the project, but icebreaking is perhaps the most significant.

U. S. Coast Guard Cutter BRAMBLE (WLB 392), 7 April 1970.

U. S. Coast Guard Cutter MAPLE (WLI 234) was built in 1939. She was stationed at Ogdensburg, New York.

U. S. Coast Guard Cutter CUYAHOGA.

U. S. Coast Guard Cutter WOODRUSH sheathed in ice.

U. S. Coast Guard Cutter OJIBWA.

U. S. Coast Guard Cutter KAW leads laker through ice.

Lake freighter in rough weather on Lake Huron.

81

Icebreaking services for the Great Lakes region are provided primarily by two large icebreakers, MACKINAW, specially-built for Great Lakes use and the polar class WESTWIND. In addition, numerous smaller vessels are employed in rivers and narrow channels to maintain traffic flow.

Between mid and late December, as ice begins to form rapidly on the Lakes, especially in shallow waters, three operations move into gear almost simultaneously. These are called "Taconite", "Coal Shovel" and "Oil Can" and they support the shipment of the types of products which their names suggest.

Under the direction of Coast Guard Group, Sault Ste. Marie, Michigan, icebreaking for the Taconite Operation is centered mainly in Whitefish Bay, the St. Mary's River and the Straits of Mackinac. In support of this operation, the Coast Guard's primary resource is the 290-foot MACKINAW and the polar icebreaker WESTWIND. Their job is to keep the shipping lanes open for ore boats carrying taconite from the port of Two Harbors, Minnesota to steel mills in Chicago and Gary. The big 'breakers are assisted by the 180-foot WOODRUSH, a Duluth-based buoy tender and the 110-foot tugs NAUGATUCK and ARUNDEL from Sault Ste. Marie and Chicago, and SUNDEW from Charlevoix, Michigan.

U. S. Coast Guard Cutter NAUGATUCK.

Commencing at about the same time as Operation Taconite, Operation Coal Shovel aims at insuring the uninterrupted shipment of coal from the southern shore of Lake Erie, primarily Toledo, to the factories and power plants of the Detroit area. In Coal Shovel, the responsibilities of icebreaker assistance are borne entirely by smaller cutters, specifically the buoy tenders ACACIA and MARIPOSA and the tugs KAW and OJIBWA.

A third operation involving the cutters MESQUITE from Sturgeon Bay, Wisconsin and RARITAN from Grand Haven, Michigan known as "Oil Can" assists tankers in the Green Bay and Grand Traverse Bay areas.

U. S. Coast Guard Cutter ARUNDEL.

In winters when the weather is especially severe, the prevailing northwesterly winds create ice build-ups in several areas of the lakes and rivers. Lake Erie's eastern end is highly susceptible to this type of buildup and is the work area for "Operation Open Buffalo". This operation marks the spring opening of the St. Lawrence Seaway. The cutters KAW and OJIBWA and, if warranted, one of the big

U. S. Coast Guard Cutter RARITAN.

'breakers, are the workhorses for this task. "Open Buffalo" was not employed during the winters of 1974-76.

The nerve center for the Coast Guard's ice operations on the Great Lakes is the Ice Navigation Center (INC), located in the Ninth Coast Guard District Headquarters in Cleveland, Ohio. Here, information from dozens of sources is collected, analyzed and disseminated back to the shipping companies, ships underway and the government agencies involved in the Extension Program. Ice information is provided by forty eight Coast Guard shore units, aerial reconnaissance flights from bases in Traverse City, Cleveland, and Chicago, ships underway in the ice fields and a variety of other sources, including the Canadian Ice Central at Ottawa, Quebec.

A National Weather Service Ice Forecaster is assigned to the Ice Navigation Center providing a unique blending of personnel from two agencies at one location, working in harmony to accomplish a single mission. Considerable weather information flows into the Ice Center from around the Lakes and the Nation. The two standard National Weather Service teletype circuits, are an integral part of the Center's equipment and a receiver on the weather map fascimile circuit connects it with the National Meteorological Center near Washington, D. C. A special marine weather data teletype circuit provides the link between the Ice Center and United States and Canadian Forecast Offices, major users and marine radio stations. The teletype circuit and a direct facsimile line also link INC with another ice forecaster at the National Weather Service Forecast Office in Detroit.

This year, a new information gathering device has been added to the program. Operation of the device, known as Side-Looking Airborne Radar (SLAR) is a cooperative effort involving personnel from the U. S. Coast Guard, National Aeronautics and Space Administration (NASA), National Weather Service (NWS), and the Lorain Electronics Corporation (MARAD Network). The SLAR apparatus records and transmits data to be evaluated and retransmitted to mariners of the Great Lakes, permitting them to make their runs through the ice in the path of least resistance.

Summarized briefly, the NASA equipment, mounted onboard a Coast Guard HC-130 aircraft emits a signal, uninterfered by rain, snow, fog or heavy clouds. The signal is

bounced from the ice, received and decoded by equipment on the aircraft while simultaneously being bounced via SMS/GOES (Geosynchronous Orbit Earth Satellite) to the Ice Navigation Center in Cleveland. Upon receiving the radar imagery, the staff of the Ice Navigation Center makes a graphic analysis of the ice patterns tracing the ice fields on a base map and adding thickness and ice "type" data. These findings are then transmitted via special telephone lines to Lorain Electronics Corporation for further transmission to mariners equipped with facsimile recorders.

Another key element of the ice information network is the use of an airborne S-Band (2.8 GHz) short-pulse radar system which measures actual ice thicknesses with an accuracy of about two inches from an altitude of 4,500 feet.

Research and development projects are also an important part of the Coast Guard's efforts in the Extension of the Season Program. One such project is being conducted to measure the forces of ice on aids to navigation structures to determine the adequacy of existing devices and aid in the development of new concepts. A program to assess the adequacy of shipboard escape and survival systems during an extended season is also an area of major concern to the Coast Guard.

All of these efforts combined with comparatively mild winters during 1974-76 have enabled Great Lakes mariners to operate their vessels throughout both winters with only minor delays due to ice and weather.

U. S. Coast Guard Cutter WESTWIND breaking ice. (Photo by The Detroit News.)

HU-16E Grumman Albatross before introduction of the Coast Guard slash.

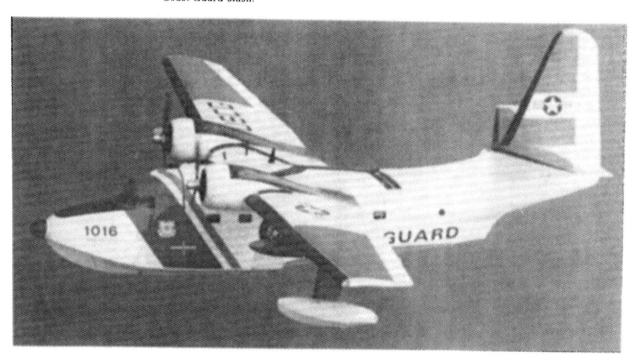

HU-16 Grumman Albatross with the Coast Guard slash.

HH-52A in flight.

H04S Helicopter landing on flight deck of U. S. Coast Guard Cutter MACKINAW (WAGB 83).

U. S. Coast Guard Cutter MACKINAW.

U. S. Coast Guard Cutter SOUTHWIND opens a track for
the Enders M. Voorhees, January 1974.

85

APPENDIX I

Ninth District Commanders

Captain Ralph W. Dempwolf	1942 - 1944
Commodore J. A. Hirshfield	1944 - 1950
Rear Admiral R. L. Raney	9/02/50 - 8/30/54
Rear Admiral Frank A. Leamy	8/31/54 - 4/21/57
Rear Admiral Edward H. Thiele	4/22/57 - 7/24/58
Rear Admiral Joseph A. Kerrins	9/25/58 - 4/29/60
Read Admiral George H. Miller	4/29/60 - 6/30/64
Rear Admiral Chester R. Bender	6/22/64 - 6/15/65
Rear Admiral Willard J. Smith	7/28/65 - 3/31/66
Rear Admiral Charles Tighe	5/06/66 - 7/01/68
Rear Admiral W. F. Rea, III	6/24/68 - 7/01/70
Rear Admiral William A. Jenkins	7/01/70 - 4/05/72
Rear Admiral A. A. Heckman	4/05/72 - 8/74
Rear Admiral J. S. Gracey	8/74 - Present

Rear Admiral James S. Gracey, Commander, Ninth Coast Guard District, September 1974 to present.

Rear Admiral Roy L. Raney, Commander, Ninth Coast Guard District, September 1950 through August 1954.

Coast Guard 44-footer in heavy seas of Lake Erie.

APPENDIX II

LISTING OF
UNITS IN
THE
NINTH COAST GUARD DISTRICT

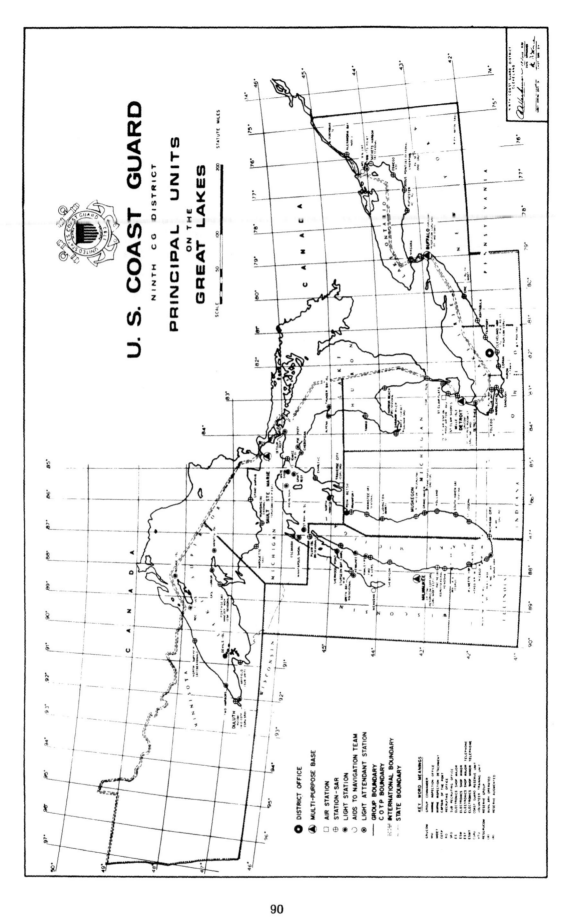

GROUPS

Commander
U. S. Coast Guard Group
1 Fuhrman Boulevard
Buffalo, New York 14203
(716) 842-2195

Commander
U. S. Coast Guard Group
2420 S. Lincoln
   Memorial Drive
Milwaukee, Wisconsin
   53207
(414) 224-3181

Commander
U. S. Coast Guard Group
Foot of Mt. Elliott Ave.
Detroit, Michigan 48226
(313) 226-6870

Commander
U. S. Coast Guard Group
Fulton Ave. & Bluff St.
Muskegon, Michigan
   49441
(616) 759-0951

Commander
U. S. Coast Guard Group
1201 Minnesota Avenue
Duluth, Minnesota 55802
(218) 727-6412

Commander
U. S. Coast Guard Group
Sault Ste. Marie,
   Michigan 49783
(906) 635-5242

MARINE SAFETY OFFICES

Commanding Officer
CG Marine Safety Office
Room 1111
Federal Building
111 W. Huron Street
Buffalo, NY 14202
(716) 842-2000

Commanding Officer
CG Marine Safety Office
1055 East Ninth Street
Cleveland, OH 44114
(216) 522-4405

Commanding Officer
CG Marine Safety Office
1200 Cadillac Tower Bldg.
65 Cadillac Square
Detroit, MI 48226
(313) 226-7777

Commanding Officer
CG Marine Safety Office
Federal Building
Room 501
234 Summit Street
Toledo, OH 43604
(419) 259-6372

Commanding Officer
CG Marine Safety Office
Canal Park
Duluth, MN 55802
(218) 727-6286

LIGHT STATIONS

Commanding Officer
USCG Light Station
Eagle Harbor, MI 49951
(906) 289-4433

Commanding Officer
USCG Light Station
North Manitou Shoal
Leland, MI 49654
(616) 334-3961

Commanding Officer
USCG Light Station
Rawley Point
Two Rivers, WIS 54235

Commanding Officer
USCG Light Station
Sherwood Point, Rt. 4
Sturgeon Bay, WIS 54235

Commanding Officer
USCG Light Station
Tibbets Point
Cape Vincent, NY 13618
(315) 654-4014

Commanding Officer
USCG Light Station
Manitou Island
Hancock, MI 49930
(906) 289-4569

Commanding Officer
USCG Light Station
St. Martin Island
Escanaba, MI 49829
(414) 847-2435

Commanding Officer
USCG Light Station
Passage Island
Hancock, MI 49930

Commanding Officer
USCG Light Station
Grays Reef, c/o CG Sta.
St. Ignace, MI 49781

Commanding Officer
USCG Light Station
White Shoal
c/o Coast Guard Station
St. Ignace, MI 49781

Commanding Officer
USCG Light Station
Devils Island
Bayfield, WIS 54814

Commanding Officer
USCG Light Station
Lansing Shoal
c/o CG Station
Charlevoix, MI 49720

Commanding Officer
USCG Light Station
Rock of Ages
Hancock, MI 49930

Commanding Officer
USCG Light Station
Detroit, MI 48207

Commanding Officer
USCG Light Station
Minneapolis Shoal
Escanaba, MI 49829
(906) 786-7761

Commanding Officer
USCG Light Station
Point Betsie
Frankfort, MI 49635
(616) 352-3195

Commanding Officer
USCG Light Station
Thunder Bay Island
Alpena, MI 49707
(517) 354-8881

Commanding Officer
USCG Light Station
Two Harbors
Two Harbors, MN 55616
(218) 834-3344

Commanding Officer
USCG Light Station
P. O. Box 1146
Green Bay, WIS 54305

FLOATING UNITS

Commanding Officer
USCGC ACACIA
(WLB 406)
Sturgeon Bay, WIS
54235

Commanding Officer
USCGC BUCKTHORN
(WLI 642)
c/o U. S. Coast Guard
Base
Sault Ste. Marie, MI
40700

Commanding Officer
USCGC MACKINAW
(WAGB 83)
Cheboygan, MI 49721
(616) 627-4741

Commanding Officer
USCGC OJIBWA
(WYTM 97)
c/o Coast Guard Base
1 Fuhrman Boulevard
Buffalo, NY 14203
(716) 842-2046

Commanding Officer
USCGC RARITAN
(WYTM 93)
Grand Haven, MI 49417
(616) 842-5440

Commanding Officer
USCGC PT. STEELE
(WPB 82359)
Oswego, NY 13126
(315) 343-2488

Commanding Officer
USCGC WOODRUSH
(WLB 407)
Duluth, MN 55802
Day (218) 727-6400
Night (218) 727-7928

Commanding Officer
USCGC WESTWIND
(WAGB 281)
655 East Erie Street
Milwaukee, WIS 53202

Commanding Officer
USCGC ARUNDEL
(WYTM 90)
Foot of Streeter Drive
Chicago, IL 60611
(312) 787-5181

Commanding Officer
USCGC KAW (WYTM 61)
c/o Coast Guard Station
Foot of East Ninth Street
Cleveland, OH 44114
(216) 522-4414

Commanding Officer
USCGC MARIPOSA
(WLB 397)
Foot of Mt. Elliott Ave.
Detroit, MI 48207
(313) 259-1399

Commanding Officer
USCGC NAUGATUCK
(WYTM 92)
c/o Coast Guard Base
Sault Ste. Marie, MI
49783
(906) 632-6232

Commanding Officer
USCGC SUNDEW
(WLB 404)
P. O. Box 57
Charlevoix, MI 49720
(616) 547-6766

AIR STATIONS

Commanding Officer
Coast Guard Air Station
Glenview, IL 60026
(312) 657-2145

Commanding Officer
Coast Guard Air Station
Selfridge AFB, MI 48045
(313) 465-1331

Commanding Officer
Coast Guard Air Station
Traverse City, MI 49684
(616) 946-4650

STATIONS

Commanding Officer
Coast Guard Station
Alexandria Bay, NY 13607
(315) 482-2574

Commanding Officer
Coast Guard Station
Detroit, MI 48207
(313) 331-3110

Commanding Officer
Coast Guard Station
4001 East 98th Street
Chicago, IL 60617
(312) 768-8000

Commanding Officer
Coast Guard Station
1055 East Ninth Street
Cleveland, OH 44114
(216) 522-4412

Commanding Officer
Coast Guard Station
P. O. Box 8130
Erie, PA 16505
(814) 453-2215

Commanding Officer
Coast Guard Station
Frankfort, MI 49635
(616) 352-3181

Commanding Officer
Coast Guard Station
Grand Marais, MI 49839
(906) 494-2551

Commanding Officer
Coast Guard Station
2399 Ottawa Beach Rd., SW
Holland, MI 49423
(616) 335-5871

Commanding Officer
Coast Guard Station
Lorain, OH 44052
(216) 288-1206

Commanding Officer
Coast Guard Station
P. O. Box 27
Manistee, MI 49660
(616) 723-7412

Commanding Officer
Coast Guard Station
Ashtabula, OH 44004
(216) 964-9417

Commanding Officer
Coast Guard Station
1201 Minnesota Avenue
Duluth, MN 55802
(218) 727-6412

Commanding Officer
Coast Guard Station
Grand Haven, MI 49417
(616) 842-2510

Commanding Officer
Coast Guard Station
Harbor Beach, MI 48441
(517) 479-2685

Commanding Officer
Coast Guard Station
Kenosha, WIS 53140
(414) 657-7651

Commanding Officer
Coast Guard Station
Charlevoix, MI 49720
(616) 547-2541

Commanding Officer
Coast Guard Station
Grand River, Ohio 44045
(216) 352-3111

Commanding Officer
Coast Guard Station
Ludington, MI 49431
(616) 843-9088

Commanding Officer
Coast Guard Station
Marblehead, OH 43440
(419) 798-4444

Commanding Officer
Coast Guard Station
Marquette, MI 49855
(906) 226-3312

Commanding Officer
Coast Guard Station
c/o CG Group
2420 S. Lincoln
Memorial Dr.
Milwaukee, WIS 53207
(414) 224-3167

Commanding Officer
Coast Guard Station
Muskegon, MI 49441
(616) 759-8581

Commanding Officer
Coast Guard Station
Washington Island,
  WIS 54246
(414) 847-2215

Commanding Officer
Coast Guard Station
Port Huron, MI 48060
(313) 984-2602

Commanding Officer
Coast Guard Station
Rochester, NY 14617
(716) 342-4140

Commanding Officer
Coast Guard Station
Station A
Bay City, MI 48706
(517) 684-3343

Commanding Officer
Coast Guard Station
24802 E. Jefferson Ave.
St. Clair Shores,
  MI 48080
(313) 778-0590

Commanding Officer
Coast Guard Station
127 N. Pier Street
P. O. Box 500
St. Joseph, MI 49085

Commanding Officer
Coast Guard Station
Wilmette, IL 60091
(312) 251-0185

Commanding Officer
Coast Guard Station
Michigan City, IND 46360
(219) 879-8371

Commanding Officer
Coast Guard Station
Youngstown NY 14174
(716) 745-3327

Commanding Officer
Coast Guard Station
Oswego, NY 13126
(315) 343-1551

Commanding Officer
Coast Guard Station
St. Clair Flats
Harsens Island, MI 48028
(313) 748-9921

Commanding Officer
Coast Guard Station
St. Ignace, MI 49781
(906) 643-9191

Commanding Officer
Coast Guard Station
Sheboygan, WIS 53081
(414) 452-5115

Commanding Officer
Coast Guard Station
East Tawas, MI 48730
(517) 362-4428

Commanding Officer
Coast Guard Station
Two Rivers, WIS 54241
(414) 793-1304

Commanding Officer
Coast Guard Station
Sturgeon Bay, WIS 54235
(414) 743-3366

Commanding Officer
Coast Guard Station
Bay View Park
Toledo, Ohio 43611
(419) 250-6447

"Activities of the United States Coast Guard Upon the Great Lakes During 1941". *Coast Guard Bulletin* Vol. 1 No. 35 (May 1942) and Vol. 1 No. 36 (June 1942)

Adams, E. P. "Lighthouse System of the United States". *Journal of Association of Engineering Societies* Vol. 12 No. 10 (October 1893) pp. 509-31

Adamson, Hans Christian. *Keepers of the Lights.* New York: Greenberg, 1955

Baarslag, Karl. *Coast Guard to the Rescue.* New York: Farran & Rinehart, Inc., 1937

Barnett, J. P. *The Lifesaving Guns of David Lyle.* South Bend, Indiana: South Bend Replicas, Inc., 1976

Boelio, Bob. "Sentinels of the Lakes" *Motor News: Official Publication of the Automobile Club of Michigan* Vol. 46 No. 12 (June 1964) p. 12

Bibb, A. B. "The Life-Saving Service on the Great Lakes". *Frank Leslie's Popular Monthly* Vol. XIII (April 1882) pp. 386-98

Boyce, Daron. "Great Lakes Ice Navigation Center". *Mariners Weather Log* Vol. 18 No. 1 (January 1974) pp. 17-22

Brotherton, R. A. "The Wreck of the Kershaw and Kent". *Inland Seas: Quarterly Journal of the Great Lakes Historical Society* Vol. 4 No. 2 (Summer 1948) pp. 124-26

Cairo, Lieutenant Commander Robert F., USN. "Notes on Early Lightship Development". *Coast Guard Engineer's Digest,* No. 188 (July-August-September 1975) pp. 3-12

Carpenter, F. G. "United States Life Saving Service". *Popular Science Monthly* Vol. 44 (January 1894) p. 346

Castle, Beatrice Hanscom. *The Grand Island Story* Marquette, Michigan: John M. Longyear Research Library, 1974

Claudy, C. H. "Lighthouse Service of the United States". *World Today,* Vol. 12 (May 1907) pp. 536-46

"Coast Guard Planning New Ice Breaker for the Great Lakes". *Coast Guard Bulletin,* Vol. 1 No. 30 (December 1941) p. 239

Connelly, Will. *Downriver Michigan: Ice Age to Today,* Wyandotte, Michigan: The Connelly Company, 1976

Cox, Samuel Sullivan. "Life Saving Service". *North American Review* Vol. 132 (May 1881) p. 482

Dancy, Thomas B. "Twin Strandings at Ludington". *Inland Seas: Quarterly Journal of the Great Lakes Historical Society* Vol. 3 No. 2 (April 1947) pp. 59-65

Davis, Rebecca Harding "Life Saving Stations". *Lippincott's Magazine* Vol. XVII (March 1876) p. 301-10

Denty, Captain S. L., USCG. "The Coast Guard: A Brief Resume of Its History and Functions". Address before the Cleveland Engineering Society, March 13, 1956

Doughty, Francis Albert. "Life At A Life Saving Station". *Catholic World* Vol. 65 (July 1897) p. 514-27

Ehrhardt, John B. *Joseph Francis 1801-1893: Shipbuilder: Father of the U. S. Life-Saving Service.* Princeton, N. J.: Printed by the Princeton University Press for the Newcomen Society, 1950

Eldridge, F. R. *"They Have To Go Out": Historical Sketch of the U. S. Coast Guard 1790-1946.* Washington: Historical Section, Public Information Division, U. S. Coast Guard Headquarters, 1953

Evans, Captain Stephen H., USCG. *The U. S. Coast Guard 1790-1915.* Annapolis, Md: U. S. Naval Institute, 1949

Freeman, Rev. T. J. A., S. J. "The Life-Saving Service of the United States". *American Catholic Quarterly Review* Vol. 18 (July 1893) p. 650-66

Frederickson, Arthur C., and Lucy F. "Gallant Men of the Sea". *Ships and Shipwrecks In Door County Wisconsin* Vol. II. Sturgeon Bay, Wisconsin: Door County Publishing Co., 1963

Gerred, Janice H. "Wreck of the Alex Nimick". *Inland Seas: Quarterly Journal of the Great Lakes Historical Society* Vol. 31 No. 2 (Summer 1975) p. 139

Glaza, Chief Boatswain (L) A. F., USCG. "Great Lakes Hazards". *The U. S. Coast Guard Magazine* Vol. 5 No. 1 (November 1931) p. 12-15

Gobble, Ensign Richard G., USCG. "Tough, Dangerous Work". *Lakeland Boating: Mid-America's Freshwater Yachting Magazine,* Vol. XX No. 4 (May 1965) p. 8

Grupp, George W. "The First Child Is Born In Steam Launch to Michigan Lighthouse Keeper". *Navy Times,* December 3, 1955

Hamilton, Frank E. "A Forgotten Port and Log Towing Revenue Cutters". *Telescope: Great Lakes Maritime Institute, Dossin Great Lakes Museum,* Vol. 18 No. 1 (January-February 1969) p. 206-11

Heckman, Rear Admiral A. A., USCG. "Remarks Given At Official Transfer of U. S. C. G. Rifle Range Property to City of Ferrysburg, Michigan". Cleveland, Ohio, 1973

Heller, Robert. "The Great Lakes Region: A Maritime Appraisal". Lecture of the Newcomen Society in North America. U. S. Coast Guard Academy, New London, Connecticut, October 16, 1962

House, Captain Roscoe, USCG. "Progress In Aids To Navigation". Paper, Cleveland, Ohio, undated

Hoyt, Roscoe. "Ninth District Radio". *The U. S. Coast Guard Magazine* Vol. 5 No. 1 (November 1931) p. 40

Imlay, Rear Admiral Miles, USCG(Retired). "The Story of the Lifecar". *Alumni Association Bulletin* Vol. XX No. 3-4 (July-August 1958) pp. 52-62

Ingraham, Rex. *First Fleet, The Story of the U. S. Coast Guard At War.* New York: The Bobbs-Merrill Company, 1944

Jenkins, Rear Admiral W. A., USCG. Remarks at Change of Command Ceremony, Ninth Coast Guard District, March 29, 1972, Cleveland, Ohio, 1972

———— Remarks at Dedication Ceremony Alexandria Bay, New York on September 5, 1970. Cleveland, Ohio, 1970

Jenks, William Lee. *St. Clair County, Michigan: Its History and Its People,* Vol. I

Johnson, Arnold Borges, Chief Clerk, U. S. Light-house Board. *The Modern Light-House Service.* Washington: U. S. Government Printing Office, 1890

Johnson, Harvey F. "Engineering; Legare '44 to Escanaba '32". *The U. S. Coast Guard Magazine* Vol. 6 (March 1933) p. 2

Johnson, Lieutenant S. B., USCG. "District Duties Vary". *The U. S. Coast Guard Magazine* Vol. 5 No. 1 (November 1931) pp. 26-28

Johnson, Theodore. "The Life-Saving Service of the Lakes—The Relation of Captain Dobbins Thereto". *Magazine of Western History* Vol. 4 (June 1886) p. 226

Kaler, J. O. *Lightkeepers of the U. S. Lighthouse Service.* New York: E. P. Dutton & Company, 1906

Kaplan, H. R. and Lieutenant Commander J. F. Hunt, USCG. *This Is The Coast Guard.* Cambridge, Maryland: Cornell Maritime Press, Inc., 1972

Kimball, Sumner Increase, General Superintendent of the U. S. Life Saving Service. "Organization and Methods of the United States Life Saving Service" Report. Read to the Committee on Life-Saving Systems and Devices, International Marine Conference, November 22, 1889.

Lamb, M. J. "The American Life Saving Service". *Harper's New Monthly Magazine* Vol. LXIV No. CCCLXXXI (February 1882) pp. 357-73

Law, Rev. William Hainstock. *Deeds of Valor by Heroes and Heroines of the Great Water World.* Detroit: Pohl Printing Company, 1911

—— *Heroes of the Great Lakes With An Account of the Recent Great Disasters.* Detroit: Pohl Printing Co., 1906

—— *Important Light Towers In The Great Water World.* Detroit: Pohl Printing Company, 1915

—— *"The Life Savers in the Great Lakes": Incidents and Experiences Among the Life Savers in Lake Huron and Lake Superior (known as District 11).* Detroit: Winn & Hammond, 1902

"Life Saving Service of the United States". *American Architect,* Vol. 16, (September 13, 1884) p. 124

"Lights On Our Lakes". *The Interlake Log* (November 1970) pp. 3-7

Little, C. H. "Naval Activities on the Great Lakes: Past and Present". *Canadian Geographical Journal* Vol. 67, No. 6 (December 1963) pp. 202-215

Macy, Robert H. "Consolidation of the Lighthouse Service with the Coast Guard". *U. S. Naval Institute Proceedings* Vol. 66 (January 1940) p. 58

Mansfield, J. B. *History of the Great Lakes.* Chicago: J. H. Beers & Co., 1899, 2 Volumes

Marquette, Michigan Historical Society. "Life Saving Station in Marquette" (by Kenyon Boyer)

McCain, John W. Jr. "The Beach Patrol and a Great Tradition". *United States Naval Institute Proceedings* Vol. 70, No. 9 (September 1944) p. 1123-27

McLellan, Captain C. H., USRCS. "The Evolution of the Lifeboat". *Marine Engineering* (January 1906) pp. 7-11

"Modern Mariner, The". *Light Magazine* Vol. 39, No. 1 (1970)

Moore, Mary Jane. "Tending of the Lights". *The U. S. Coast Guard Magazine* Vol. 12, No. 11 (September 1939)

Murphy, Patrick. "The Loss of Lightship No. 82". *Inland Seas: Quarterly Journal of the Great Lakes Historical Society* Vol. 31, No. 1 (Spring 1975) p. 28

Nalty, Bernard C. and Truman R. Strobridge. "Bright and Steadfast Light". *Alumni Bulletin* Vol. XXXVIII No. 6 (November-December 1975) pp. 37-41

—— "The OL-5 and the Beginnings of Coast Guard Aviation". *Journal American Aviation Historical Society* Vol. 19 No. 3 (Fall 1974) p. 200-03

—— "The U.S. Coast Guard, Midwife at the Birth of the Airplane". *Aerospace Historian* Vol. 22, No. 3 (Fall/September 1975)

Newell, W. A. *Letter From W. A. Newell, Originator of the U. S. Life Saving Service in 30th Congress to Hon. William J. Sewell—Giving Congressional History of the Origin of the Service.* Hartford, Connecticut: Press of Meyer and Noll, 1898

Noble, Dennis L. "Disaster, Heroism, and Controversy in Chicago Harbor". *Coast Guard Engineer's Digest* No. 143 (April-May-June 1974) pp. 58-62

—— "Incident In '94". *Telescope, Great Lakes Maritime Institute, Dossin Great Lakes Museum* Vol. XXIV No. 1, (January-February 1975) pp. 14-16

—— "Man the Surfboat!" *Inland Seas: Quarterly Journal of the Great Lakes Historical Society* Vol. 31, No. 3 (Fall 1975) p. 207

—— "The Old Life Saving Station at Michigan City, Indiana: 1889-1914". *Indiana History Bulletin, Indiana Historical Bureau* Vol. 51 No. 10 (October 1974) p. 136-43

—— and Mike O'Brien "Smoke and Shot". *The Chief* Vol. 2 No. 1 (January 1976) pp. 20-21

Norton, Boatswain (L) Ira B., USCG. "Personnel Problems". *The U. S. Coast Guard Magazine* Vol. 5 No. 1 (November 1931) pp. 36-37

O'Connor, W. D. "United States Life Saving Service". *Popular Science Monthly* Vol. 15 (June 1879) p. 182

O'Neill, Francis L. "A Fight Worth Winning". *The U. S. Coast Guard Magazine* Vol. 4 No. 6 (April 1931) pp. 3-4

—— "Some Jobs Well Done". *The U. S. Coast Guard Magazine* Vol. 5, No. 1 (November 1931) pp. 6-11

Pond, James L. *History of Life-Saving Appliances and Military and Naval Constructions, Invented and Manufactured by Joseph Francis, With Sketches and Incidents of His Business Life in the United States and France.* New York: E. D. Slater, 1885

Putnam, George R., Commissioner of the Lighthouse Service. *Radiobeacons and Radiobeacon Navigation.* Washington: U. S. Government Printing Office, 1931

—— *Sentinel of the Coasts: The Log of a Lighthouse Engineer.* New York: W. W. Norton & Co., Inc., 1937

Ratigan, William. *Great Lakes Shipwrecks and Survivals.* Grand Rapids, Michigan: Wm. B. Eerdmans Publishing Co., 1969

Rattray, Jeannette Edwards. "Lifesaving: New York

Area From 1848". *Perils of the Port of New York.* New York: Dodd, Mead & Company, 1973

Rea, Rear Admiral W. F. III, USCG. *Address Delivered at Dedication of the St. Ignace, Michigan Station on September 28, 1968.* Cleveland: Public Information Office, Ninth Coast Guard District, 1968

____ *Remarks on the Occasion of the Departure of the Coast Guard Cutter Tupelo from Toledo, Ohio, September 19, 1969.* Cleveland: Public Information Office, Ninth Coast Guard District, 1969

Records of Movements, Vessels of the United States Coast Guard, 1790-December 31, 1933. U. S. Coast Guard, Office of the Assistant Commandant. Washington: U. S. Coast Guard Headquarters, undated, 2 volumes

"Revenue Cutter Service, The". *Army and Navy Journal* Vol. III No. 3, Whole No. 107 (September 9, 1865) p. 46

"Revenue Service on the Lakes, The". *Army and Navy Journal* Vol. III No. 44, Whole No. 148 (June 23, 1866) p. 697

Richmond, Charlotte. "The Wreck of the Ariadne". *Shipmates* (Fall 1972) p. 15

Rouse, Edith Maude. "Captain Dobbins and His Lifeboat". *Inland Seas: Quarterly Journal of the Great Lakes Historical Society* Vol. 15, No. 1 (Spring 1959) pp. 47-48

Rozin, Skip. "Who Mourns the Vanishing Wickies?" *Audobon Magazine* (May 1972) p. 30

Sabin, L. C. "Commerce on the Lakes". *The U. S. Coast Guard Magazine* Vol. 12 No. 9 (July 1939)

Sawyer, Joan. "The Lighthouse Service". *The U. S. Coast Guard Magazine* Vol. 12 No. 10 (August 1939) pp. 6-7

Short, Lloyd M. *Steamboat-Inspection Service: Its History, Activities and Organization.* New York: D. Appleton and Company, 1922

____ *The Bureau of Navigation: Its History, Activities and Organization.* Baltimore, Maryland: The Johns Hopkins Press, 1923

Smith, Darrell Hevenor and Fred Wilbur Powell. *The Coast Guard: Its History, Activities and Organization.* Washington: The Brookings Institution, 1929

Strobridge, Truman R. "Captain Daniel Dobbins, U. S. Revenue Cutter Service—One Man History Has Forgotten". *Coast Guard Engineer's Digest,* No. 178 (January-February-March 1973)

____ "Captain Gilbert Knapp, U. S. Revenue Cutter Service: Founder of Racine, Wisconsin". *Shipmates* (Spring 1973) p. 10

____ *Chronology of Aids to Navigation and the Old Lighthouse Service 1716-1939.* Washington: Public Affairs Division, U. S. Coast Guard Headquarters, 1974

____ "The Coast Guard Emblem and Official Seal: Carrying On the Old Revenue Cutter Service Tradition." *Coast Guard Engineer's Digest* No. 179 (April-May-June 1973) pp. 46-51

____ "Early Lake Captains, Revenue Cutters, and Politics". *Inland Seas: Quarterly Journal of the Great Lakes Historical Society* Vol. 29 No. 4 (Winter 1973) p. 240-48

____ *The United States Coast Guard and the Civil War: The U.S. Revenue Marine, Its Cutters, and Semper Paratus.* Washington: Public Affairs Division, U. S. Coast Guard Headquarters, 1972

Stuart, William M. "The Great Lakes Wreck of the H. E. Runnels". *The U. S. Coast Guard Magazine* Vol. 5 (June 1932) p. 24

Talbot, Frederick A. "The Lamp-Posts of the Great Lakes of North America". *Lightships and Lighthouses.* London: William Heinemann, 1913

Thompson, P. W. "Revenue Cutter Service". *Scribner's Magazine,* Vol. 11 (February 1892) p. 207

Torbett, Joe. *Presque Isle Lighthouse.* Report. Public Information Division, U. S. Coast Guard, Washington, undated

U. S. Coast Guard. *Beach Apparatus Drill.* Washington: U. S. Government Printing Office, 1918

U. S. Coast Guard. *Guide to Historically Famous Lighthouses in the United States.* Washington: U. S. Government Printing Office, 1939

U. S. Coast Guard. *The Manual for Lifeboat Stations.* Washington: U. S. Government Printing Office, 1949

U. S. Coast Guard. Public Information Division. Historical Section. *The Coast Guard at War.* Washington: Statistical Division and Historical Section, Public Information Division, U. S. Coast Guard Headquarters, June 30, 1944-January 1, 1954, 30 volumes

U. S. Coast Guard. Public Information Division. *Coast Guard History.* Washington: U. S. Government Printing Office, 1972

U. S. Coast Guard. Statistical Division. *Sinking of the CGC Escanaba.* Washington: U. S. Coast Guard Headquarters, 1943

U. S. Department of Commerce and Labor. Bureau of Lighthouses. *Instructions to Light Keepers of the United States Lighthouse Service.* Washington: U. S. Government Printing Office, 1911

U. S. Life-Saving Service. *Annual Report of the United States Life-Saving Service.* Washington: U. S. Government Printing Office. For the years 1876 thru 1914

"United States Life Saving Service". *Republic* Vol. 5 (August 1875) p. 81

U. S. Lighthouse Establishment. *Compilation of Public Documents and Extracts from Reports and Papers Relating to Light-Houses, Light-Vessels, and Illuminating Apparatus and to Beacons, Buoys and Fog Signals 1789 to 1871.* Washington: U. S. Government Printing Office, 1871

U. S. Lighthouse Establishment. *Instructions to Light-Keepers and Masters of Light-House Vessels.* Washington: U. S. Government Printing Office, 1902

U. S. Treasury Department. *Circular Instructions of the Treasury Department Relative to the Tariff, Navigation, and Other Laws for the Year Ending December 31, 1895.* Washington: U. S. Government Printing Office, 1896

U. S. Treasury Department. Office of the Lighthouse Board. *Lighthouse Board General Orders, &c.* Washington: U. S. Government Printing Office, 1870

Vent, Myron H. *South Manitou Island: From Pioneer Settlement to Park.* Springfield, Virginia: The Goodway Press, Inc., 1973

Waldron, George V. *The Story of Thunder Bay.* Alpena, Michigan: Alpena News Publishing Company, 1911

Washington, D. C. National Archives. Record Group 26. *Circulars Relating to Administrative Matters of the Revenue Cutter Service 1841-1847,* 3 volumes

Washington, D. C. National Archives. Record Group 26. *Light-House Letters 1843-1864.*

Washington, D. C. National Archives. Record Group 26. *List of Light-House Keepers and Other Employees 1853-1868*

Washington, D. C. National Archives. Record Group 26. *Newspaper Clippings Concerning the Light-House Board and Bureau 1900-1932*

Washington, D. C. National Archives. Record Group 26. *Register of Employees of the U. S. Life-Saving Service 1866-1909,* 4 volumes

Weiss, George. *The Lighthouse Service: Its History, Activities and Organization.* Baltimore, Maryland: The Johns Hopkins Press, 1926

White, Lieutenant Richard D., USCG and Truman R. Strobridge. "Nineteenth Century Lighthouse Tenders on the Great Lakes". *Inland Seas: Quarterly Journal of the Great Lakes Historical Society* Vol. 31 No. 2 (Summer 1975)

Wolcott, Merlin D. "Heroism at Marblehead". *Inland Seas: Quarterly Journal of the Great Lakes Historical Society* Vol. 16, No. 4 (Winter 1960) p. 269

_____ "Great Lakes Lifesaving Service". *Inland Seas: Quarterly Journal of the Great Lakes Historical Society* Vol. 18 No. 1 (Spring 1962) pp. 14-21

_____ "Marblehead Lifesaving Station". *Inland Seas: Quarterly Journal of the Great Lakes Historical Society* Vol. 22 No. 4 (Winter 1966) pp. 295-300

Wolff, Julius F. Jr. "A Lake Superior Life-Saver Reminisces". *Inland Seas: Quarterly Journal of the Great Lakes Historical Society* Vol. 24 No. 2 (Summer 1968) p. 108-117

_____ "The Coast Guard Comes to Lake Superior". *Inland Seas: Quarterly Journal of the Great Lakes Historical Society* Vol. 21 No. 1 (Spring 1965) pp. 14-21

_____ "1905—Lake Superior at Its Worst". *Inland Seas: Quarterly Journal of the Great Lakes Historical Society* Vol. 18 No. 4 (Winter 1962) pp. 273-279

_____ "Some Noted Shipwrecks on the Michigan Coast of Lake Superior". *Inland Seas: Quarterly Journal of the Great Lakes Historical Society* Vol. 16 No. 3 (Fall 1960) pp. 172-79

_____ "One Hundred Years of Rescues: The Coast Guard on Lake Superior". *Inland Seas: Quarterly Journal of the Great Lakes Historical Society* Vol. 31 No. 4 (Winter 1975) p. 255 and Vol. 32 No. 1 (Spring 1976) p. 32

Zedan, Daniel J. *The History of MSO Detroit.* Report. Detroit, 1975

Printed in the United States
64552LVS00002B/458